The Complete Tax Guide for E-commerce Retailers including Amazon and eBay Sellers

D1596547

How Online Sellers Can Stay in Compliance with the IRS and State Tax Laws

WITH COMPANION CD-ROM

Martha Maeda

THE COMPLETE TAX GUIDE FOR E-COMMERCE RETAILERS INCLUDING AMAZON AND EBAY SELLERS: HOW ONLINE SELLERS CAN STAY IN COMPLIANCE WITH THE IRS AND STATE TAX LAWS — WITH COMPANION CD-ROM

Copyright © 2012 Atlantic Publishing Group, Inc.
1405 SW 6th Avenue • Ocala, Florida 34471 • Phone 800-814-1132 • Fax 352-622-1875
Website: www.atlantic-pub.com • E-mail: sales@atlantic-pub.com
SAN Number: 268-1250

Library of Congress Cataloging-in-Publication Data

Forshee, Kelly, 1986-
  The complete tax guide for eBay sellers : insider secrets you need to know / by Kelly Forshee.
     p. cm.
  Includes bibliographical references and index.
  ISBN-13: 978-1-60138-124-8 (alk. paper)
  ISBN-10: 1-60138-124-7 (alk. paper)
  1. Internet auctions. 2. Electronic commerce--Taxation--United States. 3. Small business--Taxation--United States. 4. eBay (Firm) I. Title.

  HF5478.F67 2008
  343.7306'8--dc22
                              2008015657

Printed in the United States

PROJECT MANAGER: Gretchen Pressley • gpressley@atlantic-pub.com
ASSISTANT EDITOR: Alyssa Appelman • alyssa.appelman@gmail.com
INTERIOR LAYOUT: Antoinette D'Amore • addesign@videotron.ca
PROOFREADER: C&P Marse • bluemoon6749@bellsouth.net
COVER DESIGN: Meg Buchner • meg@megbuchner.com
BACK COVER DESIGN: Jackie Miller • millerjackiej@gmail.com

Printed on Recycled Paper

A few years back we lost our beloved pet dog Bear, who was not only our best and dearest friend but also the "Vice President of Sunshine" here at Atlantic Publishing. He did not receive a salary but worked tirelessly 24 hours a day to please his parents.

Bear was a rescue dog who turned around and showered myself, my wife, Sherri, his grandparents Jean, Bob, and Nancy, and every person and animal he met (well, maybe not rabbits) with friendship and love. He made a lot of people smile every day.

We wanted you to know a portion of the profits of this book will be donated in Bear's memory to local animal shelters, parks, conservation organizations, and other individuals and nonprofit organizations in need of assistance.

– *Douglas & Sherri Brown*

PS: We have since adopted two more rescue dogs: first Scout, and the following year, Ginger. They were both mixed golden retrievers who needed a home.

Want to help animals and the world? Here are a dozen easy suggestions you and your family can implement today:

- *Adopt and rescue a pet from a local shelter.*
- *Support local and no-kill animal shelters.*
- *Plant a tree to honor someone you love.*
- *Be a developer — put up some birdhouses.*
- *Buy live, potted Christmas trees and replant them.*
- *Make sure you spend time with your animals each day.*
- *Save natural resources by recycling and buying recycled products.*
- *Drink tap water, or filter your own water at home.*
- *Whenever possible, limit your use of or do not use pesticides.*
- *If you eat seafood, make sustainable choices.*
- *Support your local farmers market.*
- *Get outside. Visit a park, volunteer, walk your dog, or ride your bike.*

Five years ago, Atlantic Publishing signed the Green Press Initiative. These guidelines promote environmentally friendly practices, such as using recycled stock and vegetable-based inks, avoiding waste, choosing energy-efficient resources, and promoting a no-pulping policy. We now use 100-percent recycled stock on all our books. The results: in one year, switching to post-consumer recycled stock saved 24 mature trees, 5,000 gallons of water, the equivalent of the total energy used for one home in a year, and the equivalent of the greenhouse gases from one car driven for a year.

Table of Contents

Chapter 2: Recordkeeping — The Basics 47

Chapter 3: Taxes That Affect Small Businesses 79

Chapter 4: Business Deductions — A Lifeline for Sole Proprietors....... 109

Chapter 5: Business Use of Your Home 139

Chapter 6: More Deductions 153

Chapter 7: How to Value Your Inventory for Taxes 165

Chapter 8: Self-Employment Taxes 175

Chapter 9: Quarterly Estimated Tax Payments 181

Chapter 10: Sales and Use Tax 187

Chapter 11: Working with a Spouse or Family Member 199

Chapter 12: Long-Term Tax Breaks: IRAs, Roth IRAs, and SEPs 209

Chapter 13: What to Do When Things Go Wrong 237

Chapter 14: Ten Biggest Tax Mistakes 247

Conclusion 251

Appendix A: Useful Websites and References............................. 253

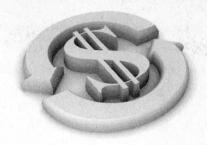

Introduction

An online marketplace is a selling platform that allows sellers to post descriptions of the items they are selling on the Internet and buyers to purchase those items with credit cards or other forms of electronic payment and have them shipped to a physical location. In just 15 years, online marketplaces have transformed the way business is done. Online shoppers easily can locate exactly what they want, compare prices, find retailers stocking the items, and have purchases conveniently delivered to their doors. Collectors and hobbyists no longer have to drive all over the country to browse through antique shops and garage sales. They can buy what they are looking for online from sellers anywhere in the world. Individuals with unique items to sell can join forces on online marketplaces with hundreds of other retailers to attract the attention of potential customers and receive credit card payments through third-party services such as PayPal.

Traffic on online marketplaces will

continue to grow as people do more of their shopping online. According to the U.S. Census Bureau, 4.4 percent of all U.S. retail sales in the last quarter of 2010 were online sales. Forrester Research predicts that this figure will grow to 8 percent by 2014.

The two largest online marketplaces, eBay and Amazon, started operating in 1994. Amazon began as an online bookseller but soon expanded its sales to many types of merchandise. In 1996, Amazon launched its Associates Program, which pays commissions to individuals who refer customers from their websites. In 1999, it set up an Amazon auction site and Amazon zShops to allow individual sellers to sell their products at fixed prices online alongside Amazon listings. One year later, zShops became Amazon Marketplace, the online selling program still in place today. At the 2010 Amazon Annual Shareholders Meeting, Jeff Bezos remarked that third-party sellers represent 30 percent of Amazon's marketplace revenue and that Amazon has 2 million active sellers.

EBay made its name as an online auction in which buyers from all over the world eagerly competed to place the winning bid in the last seconds before an auction closed, and sellers could advertise all sorts of interesting and unusual items. It is gradually shifting from an auction to fixed-price sales, as more large and mid-size retailers sell their merchandise on eBay. In April 2011,

eBay remained the largest online marketplace; it reported 95.9 million active users. During the last four months of 2010, which included the Christmas holiday season, eBay realized $1.52 billion in revenue from $15 billion in sales of merchandise through its online marketplace platforms, which include **www.eBay.com**, **www.Half.com**®, **www.Shopping.com**, and **www. Rent.com**®.

Today, individuals sell items on hundreds of online marketplaces, many of them specializing in a particular type of merchandise, such as hand-crafted goods, fine art, electronics, or used clothing. Items listed on Amazon and eBay are exposed to millions of potential customers, alongside offerings from wholesalers and major retailers. Smaller online marketplaces offer limited exposure but often for lower fees and to a more targeted audience. In addition, some major retailers, such as Sears®, Buy.com, and Walmart®, have opened marketplaces that allow individual sellers access to their online customers. Sellers also can reach customers all over the country by listing their items on classified ad sites such as Craigslist. Although many customers find the auction format exciting, the trend is toward marketplaces that allow items to be purchased immediately at fixed prices.

Taxes and the Online Marketplace — What This Means for You

Many people jump into online sales without giving much thought to keeping records or paying taxes. The publicity surrounding the 1998 Internet Tax Freedom Act, which prohibits taxation of Internet access, and the discussion of whether and when sales tax can be collected on Internet sales, has given many people the mistaken impression that profits from online sales are not subject to taxation. In fact, the Internal Revenue Service (IRS) considers cash generated from online sales taxable income. Many online sellers never have considered reporting proceeds from Internet sales on their tax returns, either because they are unaware of federal tax laws or because they think they are better off hiding this income from the IRS.

Recent changes to the tax law might have serious implications for individuals who do not report income from online sales on their tax returns. The Housing and Economic Recovery Act of 2008, scheduled to take effect in 2011, will make it easier for the IRS to identify online sellers and make sure they are correctly reporting their taxable income. One of its provisions requires processors of third-party payments and settlements, such as PayPal, Visa®, and MasterCard, to report to the IRS businesses and individuals who receive at least $20,000 a year in charges from 200 or more transactions.

PayPal will begin reporting information about high-volume, high-revenue-generating online sellers to the IRS. The IRS will then be able to check that information against the sellers' federal income tax returns to make sure the sellers reported the money generated from online sales correctly and paid taxes on that income. If a seller's tax information does not match the records, the IRS may select that individual for an audit. During the audit, the IRS will demand records and documentation related to the online sales, and the seller's entire tax year will be under scrutiny. Taxpayers who are unable to produce documents to support the claims on their federal tax returns might see their total tax liability increase. In cases where an individual is unable to produce receipts or other evidence that he or she was entitled to take certain tax deductions, taxable income may increase. A person unable to defend the claims on his or her tax return might also be liable for penalties and fines that will further increase his or her tax burden.

Though the new legislation will directly affect only those sellers who generate at least $20,000 from at least 200 transactions a year, it serves as a warning to everyone that the IRS expects online sellers to comply with federal tax laws. The IRS wants to ensure taxpayers report all income from every source. Even sellers who do not meet the $20,000 benchmark for reporting their transactions legally are required to comply with federal tax reporting requirements. If a seller's income meets the benchmark for reporting at any time in the future, the IRS may check whether that individual accurately reported all of his or her income in previous tax years. Failing to report income amounts to tax evasion, and tax evasion can incur severe penalties and fines.

You might balk at the contention that you should voluntarily provide the IRS with information that might result in your paying more taxes than if you had simply tried to hide your online sales. It is true that complying with the regulations explained in this book might result in your paying more taxes, but if you believe you can get away with not reporting the income from your online sales to the government, you might be in for a rude awakening. The IRS has every incentive to monitor online sellers and make sure they are correctly reporting their income. The IRS's job is to generate revenue for the federal government by collecting all taxes due. With Internet commerce rapidly expanding, the IRS will take a strong stance on reporting all online income. The existence of an electronic record of every online transaction dramatically decreases the chances you will get away with failing to report the income from your online sales. If you are thinking of ignoring tax laws, consider that when you are caught, the price you pay will be much higher than the amount of your past-due taxes. The IRS imposes high penalties and fees, and individuals who intentionally fail to report taxable income and pay the required taxes can face criminal charges.

How penalties and fees can add to your tax burden

The **Internal Revenue Code (IRC)** contains several penalty provisions. The amount of a penalty can range from 0.5 percent of the tax owed on an individual's tax return to 75 percent of the amount that an individual failed to report on his or her tax return. The following example is an illustration of how you can be penalized for intentionally failing to report income on your tax return:

 Mary Ellen works as a mechanic and runs a profitable business selling antique dolls on eBay. In 2009, she made $12,000 net profit from the sale of antique dolls through her eBay business and took home $35,000 from her work as a mechanic. On her 2009 federal tax return, Mary Ellen reported the $35,000 of income from her work as a mechanic but did not report the $12,000 from her eBay sales. She knew that she should have reported the $12,000 but left it off the return because she figured the chances of the IRS finding out about that amount were slim, and she did not want to pay taxes on the amount. Unfortunately, the IRS audited Mary Ellen's 2009 tax year and discovered that she attempted to conceal the $12,000 in profit from her eBay sales.

Because Mary Ellen intentionally left the $12,000 off her federal tax return in an attempt to pay less tax, the IRS levied a fraud penalty against her. A fraud penalty is imposed by the IRS against a taxpayer who commits fraud by intentionally underpaying his or her taxes. When a taxpayer purposefully decides to leave income off a tax return, he or she pays less tax than if he or she had included the income. The fraud penalty is 75 percent of the amount of the fraudulent underpayment.

Assume that Mary Ellen is in the 20-percent tax bracket. *This will be explained further in Chapter 4.* By intentionally failing to report the $12,000 of income, Mary Ellen underreported her taxes by $2,400 ($12,000 of income x 0.20 rate of tax = $2,400 tax liability). This is the amount of the fraudulent underpayment. The fraud penalty will be 75 percent of the fraudulent underpayment, which in this case would be $1,800 ($2,400 x 0.75 = $1,800). Mary Ellen will be responsible for the fraud penalty ($1,800) in addition to the $2,400 of tax she must pay on the $12,000 of income. This results in a total bill of $4,200. Compare this to the tax bill of $2,400 if Mary Ellen had included the income on her return.

The IRS requires you to pay income tax on your profit from online sales, but it also allows many tax deductions for owners of small businesses and for people who work out of a home office. By organizing your online sales operations as a business and by keeping proper records, you can take advantage of these deductions to reduce your taxable income. Take some time to learn about operating a business, and plan carefully right from the start, so you can receive the maximum benefit while complying with federal tax laws. A good system of keeping records and accounts not only helps you avoid an audit by the IRS; it is essential for running a profitable business. When you regularly track your sales and expenses, you will discover ways to shave costs, cut your losses, increase sales, and expand your business with new marketplaces and successful new products.

Failure to report taxable income on your federal tax return is not the only way you can run afoul of the law with an Internet business. In many areas, you must pay state and local income taxes in addition to the federal tax. If you are selling to retail customers, you are also expected to collect and pay sales tax. Cities and counties have laws and ordinances requiring local business owners to register their businesses and follow zoning restrictions. Internet marketplaces have their own sets of rules regarding what can be sold and how transactions are carried out. Not complying with these requirements could result in fees and penalties, and you could even be forced to shut down your business.

Selling your used treadmill does not incur a tax liability

When you sell something that you bought and no longer need, you do not need to pay tax on the income because you are selling it for less than what you originally paid for it. That is considered a personal loss.

This book is your guide to navigating the complexities of tax laws and business regulations. Here you will find all the information you need to avoid getting into trouble with the IRS and state and local taxing authorities and reap the maximum benefits from tax deductions. Understand the logic behind tax codes. Learn to set up your online retail sales operation as a business so you can claim tax deductions to reduce your taxable income. Find out how and when sales tax is collected on Internet sales, how to file tax returns, and how to calculate and pay sales tax. Review basic accounting principles and the software programs available for bookkeeping and recordkeeping. Learn how to calculate your profit on used books, antiques, and collectibles that you find around your home or at garage sales and flea markets. Finally, learn what to do if you are selected for an IRS audit, or when you find that you owe sales taxes or taxes on income from previous years.

At the end of the book, you will find a list of useful websites where you can find additional information and a glossary of commonly used terms.

CHAPTER 1

A Hobby or a Business?

Some people post a few items that they no longer need or use, such as outgrown baby furniture, textbooks, or musical instruments, on an online marketplace to make some extra money. Others use online marketplaces to buy and sell rare or collectible items, such as toys, dolls, or car parts for restoring vintage automobiles. The money they make from selling one item often goes toward buying other items they want to collect or resell. Activities of these types are regarded as hobbies rather than businesses because the sellers are more interested in acquiring or selling specific items than in making a regular income.

However, for millions of other people, selling items on the Internet has become a profitable exercise that brings in hundreds or thousands of dollars per month. In either case, the profits a seller generates are taxable income. Both the casual seller and the professional seller must report profits from sales as income on their federal tax returns.

When hobby sellers are casting around for ways to reduce their taxable income at tax time, they often consider reporting expenses associated with online sales as business expenses so they can take a larger deduction. The IRS, however, makes a distinction between business activities and sales activities that are part of a hobby.

Though the distinction between selling as a hobby or as a business does not affect whether you must report profits as taxable income, it does affect how you report this income and the kinds of tax deductions you can take. Hobby income is reported on *IRS Form 1040*. The total expenses a hobby seller can deduct from income cannot exceed the amount of revenue generated by his or her online sales. Expenses that are more than the income you made from your hobby are considered personal losses and cannot be deducted from your taxable income. The hobby expenses must be itemized as a miscellaneous expense on *IRS Schedule A (Form 1040): Itemized Deductions*, and you only can deduct the amount of miscellaneous expenses (including medical expenses, charitable gifts, and mortgage interest) that exceeds 2 percent of your annual income.

A business seller, however, can deduct most of the expenses associated with selling online, as well as business losses, from his or her taxable income. Therefore, it is in your best interests to declare yourself as a business on your tax forms and take steps to make yourself such when conducting your online selling.

The Difference Between a Hobby and a Business

A hobby is an activity not engaged in for profit, while a business is an activity that is carried on with a reasonable expectation of profit. Therefore, the key distinction is the seller's intent to profit from the activity. Do you think of your online sales as a casual activity that provides you with a little extra spending money and a chance to get rid of some of your extra things, or is selling online more like a job you undertake with a business focus and a strong expectation of profit? In the latter context, profit has a professional significance that sets it apart from money generated from a casual sale. Think about why you sell online, and ask yourself, "Is this something that I do because it is fun and I like doing it, or is it something that I expect to generate a real profit? Will I continue doing this even if I do not earn money, year after year, just because I enjoy it?"

The IRS is aware that taxpayers will attempt to reduce their taxable incomes by reporting self-defined "business losses," so it has developed a procedure for determining whether a particular individual is engaged in a hobby or a business. No single factor by itself determines whether your online sales are considered a hobby or a business; the IRS looks at all the circumstances surrounding your activities. For example, a business might be expected to report losses for one or two years, but consistent losses year after year are suspect because, logically, the purpose of a business is to make money. If you intend to report your online sales as a business activity, you must establish that you are trying to make a profit.

Test your intentions

The IRS provides two ways to determine whether you are engaged in a hobby or a business. The first is an objective, bright-line (clear standard) test that you either meet or do not meet. The second is a subjective determination that requires you to look at the facts and circumstances surrounding your activity and weigh several considerations.

According to the **objective test**, an activity is a business if it generates a profit during at least three of the last five tax years, including the current year. This test, known as the "3/5 year test," is a useful way for established sellers to fall safely within the business category, but it does not apply to new sellers or those who have not generated a profit for three of the past five years. Although it is a useful test, it is not the only factor. If you do not meet this objective test, your online sales activity still could be considered a business. Individuals who do not meet the 3/5 year test must rely on the facts and circumstances discussed below to determine if their online sales are a hobby or business.

The **subjective test** requires a seller to weigh several factors to determine if he or she is engaged in a hobby or business. The IRS is looking for evidence that you treat online sales as a business and expect to generate a profit through that business. Some of the most common and relevant factors are:

o **Whether the seller conducts his or her sales in a business-like manner**
A seller who does little more than post a couple of items online each month and keeps no additional records probably is engaged in a hobby. However, a seller who advertises his or her eBay account, engages in activities to increase sales, attempts to control costs, and keeps books and records is more likely to be engaged in a business.

o **The amount of time and effort a seller spends on the activity**
The more time and effort a seller spends on Internet sales compared to other activities, the more likely it is that those sales activities are a business rather than a hobby. Someone trying to make a profit from a business will regularly devote substantial time to it. A hobbyist might neglect online sales for a week or two. If you are trying to demonstrate to the IRS that you are engaged in a business, you must be able to show you can devote a significant amount of time to it, even if you have another job.

o **The extent to which the seller depends on the income generated from the sales for his or her livelihood**
The more you depend on the income generated from your sales to support yourself or your family, the more likely it is that your online sales activity is a business rather than a hobby.

o **Whether the seller has the knowledge needed to carry on the activity as a successful business**
If you have a record of involvement in previous profit-making activities, your current online sales efforts are more likely to be a business venture. The more you know about the ins and outs of selling items online, the more likely it is that your activities are a business rather than a hobby. For example, sellers who tailor their accounts to the needs of buyers on eBay or research ways to improve the profitability of their eBay accounts demonstrate using knowledge needed to carry on eBay selling as a successful business.

o **Whether you change your methods of operation to improve profitability**
The more you respond to current conditions to improve the profitability of your account, the more likely you are to be engaged in a business rather than a hobby. A business will make adjustments and improvements, such as raising prices or dropping unpopular items, to increase its sales and profits. A hobbyist might continue the same activities year after year, even though they bring in little money. Suppose a seller of sports memorabilia realizes that signed baseballs sell significantly better than signed basketballs. After realizing this, the seller decides to reduce the number of signed basketballs in her inventory and increase the number of signed baseballs. The seller's shift to more popular inventory indicates a business activity rather than a hobby activity.

EBay Tools

Several eBay tools provide sellers with information designed to help them make the most of the marketplace. Marketplace Research, an eBay application, allows sellers to view average selling prices, hone categorical listings, track products to gauge market demand, determine seasonality of products, and design the most effective listing format. The more you use this and similar tools eBay provides, the stronger your case will be for claiming your eBay activity as a business.

o   **The amount of personal pleasure involved in the activity**

The IRS assumes that hobbies are those activities designed to generate personal pleasure while businesses are designed to generate money. This does not mean you cannot enjoy selling things online; it means you will need to demonstrate you are deriving more than enjoyment from your sales.

Helpful Resource:

The IRS explains the rules for determining if an activity is a hobby or business in "Business or Hobby: Answer has Implications for Deductions" on its website, **www.irs.gov/newsroom/article/0,,id=169490,00.html**.

o   **The nature of the financial losses claimed on the seller's tax return**

A startup business typically experiences substantial losses in its first year of operation, then moves closer to being profitable each year afterwards. If your losses from online sales are repeated year after year, the IRS will question whether you really intend to make a profit. Your business will be expected to make a profit in some years, even if it suffers losses in others.

Establish Yourself as a Business

If you have determined that your online sales activities constitute a business rather than a hobby, you must conduct your sales in a business-like manner. If the IRS selects you for an audit, you will be required to prove that you operate a business. As you set up your online sales accounts and conduct your sales, these are some things you can do to establish your business status as legitimate:

- Document your activities and keep accurate records.

- Write a business plan.

- Maintain a bookkeeping system, and keep receipts and official records of all your expenses.

- Open a separate business bank account and a dedicated post office box for your business.

- Create a filing system that keeps your supporting documents organized and makes it easy for you to collect information at the end of each tax year.

- Register your business and obtain licenses and permits as required by local authorities.

Write a business plan

A written business plan not only provides concrete evidence to the IRS that you are engaged in a business, but it also helps you organize your ideas, set goals, and establish benchmarks. A business plan is a short, concise document identifying your goals and setting out the steps you will take to reach them. As you work through the steps of a business plan, you will be forced to think through important details, such as how you will obtain merchandise, process payments, protect yourself from fraud, ship goods to customers, and arrange the logistics of storing and packaging. If you are still in the early stages of an online sales undertaking, your business plan will help you make important decisions. Later, you can review your business plan to see if your sales are meeting your expectations. If you are already operating your business, writing a business plan will help you form a clear picture of how well your business is doing and how you can improve it.

Your business plan can be simple or elaborate, depending on how you intend to use it. If you plan to apply for a business loan or are seeking a business partner or investor, your plan will need to contain detailed financial information, a step-by-step outline for future growth, and an exit plan explaining what will become of the business when you stop operating it. Many online sellers follow a simple business model and are not seeking outside financing; for them, a short business plan containing the elements listed below is sufficient.

You can purchase books and software programs entirely devoted to writing a successful business plan, but all of that detail is probably not necessary for an online sales business. The Small Business Administration (SBA) provides several useful resources including a tutorial "How to Write a Business Plan," on its website, **www.sba.gov/smallbusinessplanner/plan/write abusinessplan/index.html**.

Here is a simple business plan outline. *You will find a sample business plan for an online business in Appendix B and on the companion CD-ROM.*

Mission statement: Think about what you are trying to accomplish. Do you want to take a hobby and turn it into your main source of income? Are you expanding an already successful Internet sales business by adding new types of merchandise or by selling through additional marketplaces? Your mission statement is one or two paragraphs explaining the purpose of your business, what you hope to accomplish, and your attitude toward the business.

Executive summary: The executive summary contains essential information about your business, such as your target market, your qualifications and expertise, the products and services you offer, and how you plan to advertise to prospective clients. Try to define your business in a way that tells a stranger what you do.

Write the executive summary last

The executive summary is an overview of your business and is usually written after you have gone through the other components of the business plan and filled out the details. Without a detailed picture of what your business will look like, it might be difficult to adequately summarize the objectives of your business. Write the executive summary to prompt the reader to look deeper into the business plan. It is a good idea to discuss the various elements of your business plan in the order you address them in the rest of the document.

Company description: The company description contains basic information about the business itself. If someone asked you for a 30-second description of your Internet sales business, what would you tell him or her? What is the business's name? Where do you plan to conduct your business (home office, rented office, warehouse)? Will you have any employees? Are you the only owner?

Product: The product section of the business plan describes the kinds of items you plan to sell online. How and where you will acquire these items? Will you be making them yourself? If so, where will you get the supplies and materials required to produce the items?

Market analysis: The market analysis should include information about the character and nature of the online market for your product. How competitive will your product be in this market? Do other sellers on the same sales platform sell this item? Is this item easily sold online? Are there any well-established sellers on online marketplaces selling this product? What can you offer that those sellers do not offer? When putting together the market analysis section of your business plan, also consider the potential for growth in your market and whether there have been any trends lately.

Look for trends or specialties that enhance your marketability

When evaluating the market for your products, look for current trends you can take advantage of. For example, going green has recently emerged as a popular trend. Consider ways that your product line can emphasize the green movement to increase your market share. For example, if you are selling vintage clothes, you could tie them to the green concept of "reuse" by highlighting the secondhand quality of vintage. You can also enhance your marketability by specializing in a particular type of product, such as DVDs or charm bracelets, so that customers who like those items keep returning to your business.

Strategy and implementation: The strategy and implementation section of your business plan explains how you plan to achieve your business goals. How will you promote your business? How will you price your products? How many items do you plan to sell each month? How will you make your Internet sales business stand out from similar businesses? For example, you might plan an ad campaign around certain keywords, give away prizes in a monthly contest, or offer free shipping when the customer purchases more than two items. List concrete steps you can take to reach those goals.

Financial analysis: The financial analysis includes information about all the factors that will determine the financial success of your online business. How much will it cost you to acquire items you plan on selling? What are your anticipated packaging and shipping costs? How much do you need to charge for each item for you to break even? What percentage of profit do you anticipate making on each item?

A business plan is always a work in progress. Review it from time to time, adjust your goals and expectations to match what you have learned from recent experience, expand it, and update information about costs and prices. Supporting documents, such as price lists from wholesale suppliers, should be filed together with your business plan. Make copies of any contracts or agreements you enter into with online marketplaces, landlords, suppliers, or shipping companies, and attach them to your business plan. A good business plan will help you make a quick evaluation of your online business whenever necessary.

Do I need to form a business entity?

Sellers who determine that they qualify as Internet sales businesses might ask whether they need to form a business entity, such as a corporation, partnership, or limited liability company. Many Internet business sellers operate as what the IRS calls a **sole proprietorship**, a type of business entity owned and operated by one individual. Unless you plan to seek outside investors, collaborate with partners, or hire multiple full-time employees to work for you, a sole proprietorship is probably the most appropriate structure for your online sales business.

A **sole proprietorship** is owned and operated by one individual. There is no legal distinction between the individual running the business and the business itself, and earnings are treated as the owner's personal income.

The business may have its own name and its own business banking accounts, but it does not have a separate legal identity apart from its owner. When the IRS looks at a sole proprietorship, it ignores the business and looks directly at the individual running the business. Anything the business owns is treated as if the individual running the business owns it. An individual who runs a sole proprietorship reports income from the business and business losses on a *Schedule C* form attached to his or her personal income tax return *(Form 1040)*.

Sole proprietorships are cheap and easy to form, which makes them an attractive option for online sellers. You can set up a sole proprietorship, obtain licenses, and operate a business using just your first and last name. If you are planning to operate the business under your own name, you will not need to take any extra steps to form your sole proprietorship. For an online sales business, however, it is good to have a trade name that reflects the products and services you plan to offer.

The major drawback of a sole proprietorship is that the owner is liable for all of the liabilities the business generates. In the context of most online sales businesses, however, the presence of unlimited liability is not a problem because few online sellers engage in the types of behaviors that expose them to liability. Unless you are selling hazardous or illegal products, or deliberately using false advertising, a sole proprietorship is an appropriate business structure.

Other types of business entities

A **corporation** is formed by filing a document called the Articles of Incorporation with the appropriate state agency, typically the state's Office of the Secretary of State. A corporation is owned by shareholders and run by a group called the board of directors. The corporation and the shareholders each have their own legal identity. This separation of the corporate entity and the owners creates what is known as **limited liability**. Limited liability means that the shareholders are insulated from liability for most of the corporation's debts and responsibilities. Because the identity of a corporation is separate from the identity of its shareholders, corporations have two levels of tax on corporate earnings (**double taxation**): a corporate level and a shareholder level. The corporation files its own tax return and pays tax on its earnings. The shareholders pay an additional income tax on the earnings they receive from the corporation.

A **partnership** is a business entity formed when two or more people agree to carry on a business. It is helpful to think of a partnership as a contract or agreement between two or more people (the partners) to conduct a certain activity together. Unlike a corporation, a partnership may be formed by an informal agreement between two people; it is not necessary to file a formal document with the state. In a general partnership, the partners are personally responsible for all of the debts and liabilities of the partnership. There is no limited liability. Also, because the partnership does not have a separate identity like a corporation, there is no double taxation because the partnership earnings and profits "pass through" to the partners.

An **S corporation**, or small business corporation, is a corporation that elects to pass corporate income, losses, deductions, and credit through to its shareholders for federal tax purposes. S corporations have fewer than 100 shareholders.

A **limited liability company (LLC)** has elements of a both a corporation and a partnership. Like a corporation, forming an LLC requires that a document be filed with the state. The owners of an LLC are called members. Just as in a corporation, the members and company have separate legal identities, protecting members from the debts and liabilities of the company. An LLC can elect to be taxed as a partnership, in which the owners pay personal income tax on the earnings.

An LLC requires more legal paperwork than a sole proprietorship, but it gives a business owner extra protection from legal and financial liabilities. Regulations and procedures for forming LLCs differ from state to state, and they can be found in the "corporations" section of your state's secretary of state website. Two main documents normally are filed when establishing an LLC. One is an operating agreement, which addresses the management and structure of the business, the distribution of profit and loss, the method of voting, and how changes in the organizational structure will be handled. The operating agreement is not required by every state. Articles of Organization, however, are required by every state, and the required form generally is available for download from your state's website. The purpose of the Articles of Organization is to establish your business legally by registering with your state. It must contain, at a minimum, the following information:

- The limited liability company's name and the address of the principal place of business

- The purpose of the LLC

- The name and address of the LLC's registered agent (the person authorized to physically accept delivery of legal documents for the company)

- The name of the manager or managing members of the company

- An effective date for the company and signature

Register your business

You will have to register your business locally with the city or county that has jurisdiction over the area where your office is located, and you might be required to get certain licenses or permits. Failure to register your business correctly could result in fines or penalties. Every county has its own rules for business registration; contact the office of your local county clerk or look up the regulations on its website. If you are running your business out of your home, you might be required to purchase an occupational license that must be renewed every year. Typically, you fill out an application at your local city or county clerk's office and pay a fee. After the zoning department determines that your business complies with local zoning laws, you will be issued a license. If you are using an assumed name for your business, make sure the correct name is listed on the registration.

You can use the SBA.gov's *Search for Business Licenses and Permits* online **(www.sba.gov/content/search-business-licenses-and-permits)** to get a list of the federal, state, and local permits, licenses, and registrations you will need to operate your business.

Many local jurisdictions have zoning restrictions, and even the rules of your homeowner's association could affect you if you plan to conduct your business in a residential area. For example, there may be a limit to the number of employees who can work with you in your home, parking restrictions, limitations on delivery trucks, and prohibitions against storing merchandise in your home or garage. Your local Small Business Administration can advise you about the licenses you need for the specific state and zone in which you live.

State Licenses

Some states require additional licenses to start a business or sell certain types of goods, such as handmade foods or cosmetics, or vitamin supplements. Most of these licenses are required only if the goods being sold could cause harm to another person, and most online auction sites restrict the sale of such items.

Auctioneer license

Some states require you to have an auctioneer license to sell goods through online auction sites, particularly if you are a "trading assistant" (**http://ebay-tradingassistant.com**) selling goods on behalf of other people for a commission or fee. Examples are the iSold It® stores (**http://877isoldit.com/products-services/auction-services.asp**) or eBay Drop Off stores where individuals can drop off items to be sold on eBay. EBay actively opposes the imposition of such laws because transactions on eBay are fundamentally different from traditional auctions. Auctioneer licenses are intended to prevent the sale of stolen goods and to give consumers recourse if they are taken advantage of in an auction, but online auction platforms automatically offer a degree of consumer protection. In traditional auctions, payment is held in escrow until a transaction is concluded; in online auctions, there is no need for this because the payment goes directly to the seller. Most states no longer have these laws, but in some states, they still exist.

EBay Main Street

EBay Main Street (**www.ebaymainstreet.com**) is a grassroots network of eBay sellers who are kept informed of legislative matters that might affect e-commerce and users of eBay, PayPal, and StubHub and other eBay Inc. companies. Its members are sometimes asked to write to their legislators or participate in lobbying activities.

EBay Main Street has campaigned against laws or proposed laws in Pennsylvania, California, Tennessee, Illinois, Florida, and Texas requiring their sellers to get auctioneers licenses. In Ohio, after much protest, eBay sellers were exempted from a law passed in March 2005 that required them to have an auctioneer license to be able to sell goods on eBay as a business.

In some states, an auctioneer license is relatively inexpensive and easy to obtain, but in others, it can cost as much as $1,000 annually and require the candidate to undergo a year of apprenticeship before he or she can begin selling. If you have a business selling other peoples' items on online auction sites, find out what the laws are in your state. That information is available from the Office of the Attorney General in most states and from some state auction boards. The A1 Auctions.com website, **www.a1auctions.com/licensing.htm#top**, lists the offices and phone numbers where you can get information in each state. If you are already in business and do not want to risk revealing your identity, have an attorney make enquiries for you.

Reseller license or sales tax certificate

To avoid paying sales tax on merchandise you purchase from wholesalers, you will need to obtain a permit, typically called a reseller's license or a sales tax certificate, from the State Department of Treasury, State Department of Taxation, or State Department of Revenue in your state. This license gives you the right to buy goods to sell from a wholesaler tax-free. You will be expected to collect and pay sales tax when you resell the goods to retail customers. *Chapter 10 discusses sales tax in detail.*

Select a Name for Your Business

One of the first impressions customers shopping online get of your business is its name at the bottom of your listing. A professional-sounding name inspires confidence and gives the impression that you seriously are committed to giving reliable service. It also is easier to remember if a customer is satisfied with the first purchase and wants to buy something else from you. For example, "Apple Dapple Confections" sounds more fun and exciting than "Mike Smith."

Many people who start a small business have a name picked out long before they make a serious start on the paperwork. Your company's name should be catchy or memorable. Short is better than long, and alliteration or some rhyming is often helpful. Putting two words together is an oft-used technique (such as Walmart, which is named after its founder Sam Walton, and mart, meaning "market"). A certain amount of misspelling is tolerated in business names, but do not carry this too far. Avoid names that have meaning only for one nationality, culture, or regional location unless your business caters to that group or locality. Check around to make sure there are no business names similar to yours that will cause confusion for your customers. Keep in mind that your business name will be tied to your online store name (when you set one up), so it needs to be something that will be easily remembered by your online customers.

Once you select a trade name for your Internet sales business, you will need to register it with your state. As soon as you have decided on a name, claim it. If you are using it as the name of your corporation, file your incorporation documents as soon as possible. If you are a sole proprietorship or partnership, register it as an assumed name (fictitious name) with the Office of the Secretary of State in your state and locally with your county clerk. The only states that specifically do not require any type of filing when conducting business under a different name are: Alabama, Arizona, Kansas, Mississippi, New Mexico, and South Carolina. Washington, D.C. makes it optional, and Tennessee does not require such filing for sole proprietorships or general partnerships.

Conduct a thorough search to confirm no one else is using the name. Start with the Yellow Pages and the Internet. Type the name into several Internet search engines, including Google (**www.google.com**), Microsoft's Bing™ (**www.bing.com**), and DMOZ Open Directory Project (**http://dmoz. org**). Before you can register your company name with the secretary of state's office in your state, you must prove no other business in that state is using the same name. Most of the state websites where you can submit a business name registration begin with a name search of all businesses registered in that state. Your local county clerk has a record of all the fictitious names (or assumed names) registered in your county.

Claim an Internet domain name

Check to see if your business name, or something similar to it, is available as an Internet domain name. Your website will be an important marketing tool for your business; many potential clients will visit your website before they make a purchase. You can search for available domain names on the InterNIC website: **http://internic.net/whois.html**. Register your domain name immediately with an inexpensive registrar, such as GoDaddy.com˚ (**www.godaddy.com**) or Network Solutions˚ (**www.networksolutions.com**), along with possible misspell ings and obvious variations. Each domain name costs only $7 to $10 per year (some of the new suffixes cost more). When you set up your website, you can arrange for all of these other domain names to redirect to your site. Be sure to renew your domain names on time or set up automatic renewals so you do not lose the investment you have made in your website later on.

Design a Logo for Your Business

Your logo, like your name, is a visual symbol that instantly identifies your business. Just like the words in a name, the colors and forms of a logo convey specific feelings and messages. A logo can be your company name or initials, a simple shape, or an elaborately designed symbol. Even if you have already designed your logo, it is a good idea to get a graphic designer to create it for you using illustration software so you will have high-quality images to use in print and on

websites. A professional artist will make sure your logo design is balanced and aesthetically pleasing. If you cannot afford to hire a professional, look for a student or a friend who has experience with graphic design software. Or do it yourself using the logo design tools on Guru Corporation's LogoSnap.com (**www.logosnap.com**) or HP's LogoMaker (**http://logomaker. com**). Your logo will appear on business cards and letterhead stationery, reports for clients, on your website, and on all of your products. Many social media sites and websites allow you to display a thumbnail of your logo alongside a link to your site so potential customers can identify you at a glance, without even reading your name.

Open a Bank Account

If you are operating as a sole proprietorship, you are not required to have a separate business bank account. You might not want to pay the fees to maintain a separate business account until you have regular business income. As soon as your business grows to the point where your personal finances must be kept separate from your business finances, a business bank account will be necessary. A partnership, LLC, or corporation should have a bank account in its name.

Before going into a bank to open a business account, compare fees and services for business bank accounts by calling local banks or looking on their websites. Meet with a bank representative when you go to open a business checking account, and inquire about the services available for businesses, such as online banking, business credit cards, and business lines of credit. (A line of credit account is an arrangement whereby the bank extends a specified amount of unsecured credit to the borrower.) Some banks occasionally offer cash in your account or other incentives to open a business account. When you speak to the bank's customer service representative, you might be able to secure additional services, such as free checks, advertised by the bank's competitors.

To establish a business checking account, most financial institutions will require a copy of the state's certificate of fictitious name filing or a business license that shows the name in which you are opening the account. To open a business checking account for a corporation, most banks will require a copy of the Articles of Incorporation, an affidavit attesting to the actual existence of the company and the employer identification number acquired from the IRS.

If you anticipate doing business with customers or suppliers outside the U.S., you might prefer a bank with a strong international department, such as Bank of America®, Wells Fargo, Global Connect, or Regions Bank, that will be able to handle and process specialized transactions, such as foreign exchange payments. Look for speed in handling transactions, electronic banking, a strong but flexible credit policy, and a solid relationship with other financial institutions overseas.

Get a Federal Tax ID Number

You can use your Social Security number (SSN) on federal tax forms if you are operating your business by yourself or with your spouse, and if the only people who work for you are independent contractors, such as freelance web designers or part-time bookkeepers. (A contractor's wages, if they exceed $600 in a single year, are reported to the IRS on *Form 1099*.) If you do not have a Social Security number, you can get one through the Social Security Administration (SSA) website, **www.ssa.gov/ssnumber**.

If you are not eligible for a Social Security number, you can get an Individual Taxpayer Identification number (ITIN) from the IRS. Apply using *Form W-7, Application for IRS Individual Taxpayer Identification Number* (**www.irs.gov/pub/irs-pdf/fw7.pdf**) or through a local IRS-authorized Acceptance Agent or IRS Taxpayer Assistance Center. For more information, see the IRS article *General ITIN Information* (**www.irs.gov/individuals/article/0,,id=222209,00.html**).

All employers, partnerships, and corporations must have an employer identification number (EIN), also known as a federal tax identification number. You must obtain your EIN from the IRS before you conduct any business transactions or hire any employees. You will also need an EIN if you are paying excise taxes on sales of tobacco products, firearms, or alcohol. (An excise tax is an additional tax levied on sales of certain goods.)

The IRS uses the EIN to identify the tax accounts of employers, certain sole proprietorships, corporations, and partnerships. The EIN is used on all tax forms and other licenses. To obtain an EIN, fill out Form SS-4, which you can obtain from the IRS at **www.irs.gov/businesses/small**. Click "Small Business Forms and Publications." There is no charge. If you are in a hurry to get your number, you can get an EIN assigned to you by telephone at (800) 829-4933. The EIN must be in the name of the person or entity that controls, manages, or directs the business and its funds and assets (known by the IRS as the "responsible party").

Get a Post Office Box

Whether you are working from a temporary office at home or have a separate physical address for your business, it is a good idea to secure a post office box at your nearest post office. That way you will not annoy your neighbors with too many package deliveries. You can rent a P.O. Box online at the U.S. Postal Service website (**www.usps.com**). Look under "All Products and Services" for "P.O. Box Service."

Having a dedicated post office box helps keep your business correspondence separate from your personal correspondence. Most important, it will prevent you from having to change your address on all your business documents and Web pages should you ever relocate your office. Continuity in any business means stability.

Online Marketplace Rules

Before jumping into the details of organizing records, you should first familiarize yourself with the rules and policies of your online marketplace(s) or auction site. Compliance with these rules is especially important for sellers engaged in an Internet sales business because the stakes are much higher for them than for casual sellers. If a casual seller's account is canceled for rules violations, he or she loses the ability to sell a couple of items and make a little extra spending money. A full-time seller whose account is canceled for violating the rules and policies loses the ability to make a living.

If the product you are planning to sell online is banned or restricted by the online marketplace, you might not be able to operate your business at all. It is also important to know how the online marketplace charges for shipping and its policies for returns and exchanges. These policies must be taken into account when you are pricing your items. You could lose money on a sale if your packing and shipping costs exceed the amount charged by

the online market-place or if you have to pay shipping costs for an item returned by a customer for an exchange or refund.

EBay's rules are typical of online market-places. They cover the following areas:

- **User Agreement**

  EBay considers agreeing to abide by the terms and conditions in the User Agreement as the most important of their requirements. The User Agreement is extensive, but a few rules are worth highlighting. First, you must be at least 18 years old to sell on eBay. Second, you agree to deliver items purchased from you as soon as the buyer complies with all posted terms. Third, the User Agreement contains the fee schedule for sellers on eBay and grants eBay the right to change the fees with 14 days notice.

- **Feedback rules**

  The Feedback rules provide guidelines for responding to feedback, requesting feedback from a trading partner, withdrawing or removing feedback, and revising feedback. Feedback can be an important tool in growing your eBay business. Sellers are encouraged to look over these rules, which can be found at **http://pages.ebay.com/help/policies/feedback-ov.html**.

- **Buyer and seller rules**

  The buyer and seller rules are designed to provide protection for buyers and sellers. They provide guidelines for etiquette and communication between buyers and sellers and outline a procedure for buyers and sellers who cannot resolve disputes related to eBay transactions to submit claims to eBay's resolution process.

- **Listing of restricted and prohibited items**

  EBay's list of restricted and prohibited items gives categories of items that are either completely prohibited from being listed or restricted in the manner in which they can be listed. These items include but are not limited to adult-only content, animal and wildlife products, counterfeit currency and stamps, drugs, event tickets, and gift cards. The complete list of prohibited and restricted items can be found at **http://pages.ebay.com/help/policies/items-ov.html**. Sellers who plan to sell any of the items on this list should make sure to comply with all relevant rules and regulations before posting such content for sale.

- **Listing rules**

  The listing rules provide a general overview of all of the rules related to listing products on eBay. These rules include the types of selling practices that are permitted on eBay, the accepted types of payments, and the details of how to list items in appropriate categories on the site. They also cover the types of links permitted in listings.

- **Intellectual property rules**

  The intellectual property rules set forth guidelines to ensure that listings do not violate the intellectual property rights of other individuals. These rules prohibit or restrict the sale of certain types of items. For example, eBay puts limits on the types of certificates of authenticity that may accompany autographed items. EBay also prohibits the sale of recordable media by individuals who do not own the copyright on such material or who are not otherwise authorized to sell the product. This second policy specifically prohibits the sale of unauthorized music compilations or bootleg videos.

EBay's website states that all users should learn eBay policies to support rules already imposed by the government and to reduce the risks to and respect the rights of buyers and sellers. EBay also states that following these rules will help users avoid having their listings, or even their memberships, suspended or canceled. All these rules can be read in their entirety on **www. eBay.com**.

Other online marketplaces, such as **www.Amazon.com** and **www.Etsy. com**, have similar policies regarding prohibited items and intellectual rights, though their fee structures and shipping arrangements may differ.

CHAPTER 2

Recordkeeping — The Basics

Keeping good records is essential to operating a successful business. Good recordkeeping allows you to monitor the progress of your business, measure your profits, identify areas where you can reduce costs, and improve procedures. Modern software programs provide you with this information instantly at any moment, giving you the ability to track sales and expenses closely and make changes before you incur big losses. Good recordkeeping is the first step to maximizing available tax benefits. It provides you with evidence to support any deductions you claim on tax returns. Accurate records show how much you have spent to acquire goods for resale and exactly how much you can claim for certain business

expenses such as vehicle mileage and office supplies. This chapter discusses the types of records and supporting documentation you will need to maintain for your business.

It is important that you learn to keep accurate records. This chapter offers some suggestions to help you get started. If you have little or no experience with accounting, assistance is available from many sources. An accountant can show you how to set up your bookkeeping system and help you file your taxes. Ask experienced online sellers to show you how they manage their accounts and recordkeeping. The Small Business Administration offers free online classes on its website, **www.sba.gov/content/recordkeeping**, as well as mentoring and training programs through its local branches (**www.sba.gov/content/find-local-sba-office**). Online sales marketplaces have tools and inexpensive third-party software applications that help keep track of expenses and provide statements and sales reports. Accounting software programs can be set up to import and organize information from your bank accounts and online sales accounts. Hire an accounting student to help you set up the software and show you how to use it. If you are overwhelmed by recordkeeping, get a part-time employee to update your accounts and file receipts. Whatever you do, do not neglect this aspect of your business.

Benefits of Recordkeeping

A good recordkeeping system keeps your business organized and saves you money and time. For example, if you promptly file invoices and packing slips from your suppliers, you will be able to look up their prices at a moment's notice and decide whether you want to order from them again. You also will be able to compare shipping costs over several months to see whether your shipping company has increased its rates. Regularly recording expenses, such as office supplies, gasoline, and boxes for packaging, and filing the associated receipts by month saves days of work when it is time to prepare your taxes. This process also ensures you do not overlook legitimate business expenses that could be deducted from your income.

Neat and efficient records will save time and make the work of your accountant much easier, if you hire one to prepare your taxes or help with your books. By keeping everything organized and in one place, you will avoid omitting important information and having to file an amended tax return.

Why the IRS thinks recordkeeping is important

Understanding how the IRS thinks about records can help you tailor your accounting system to provide the best information possible for your tax returns. The more your records correspond to IRS guidelines, the less likely you are to be audited because many of the discrepancies that trigger an audit will not be present. If you are selected for an audit, it will proceed smoothly because all the necessary documents and evidence will be easily available. The IRS gives six reasons why records are important:

- To monitor the progress of your business
- To prepare your financial statements
- To identify source of receipts
- To keep track of deductible expenses
- To prepare your tax returns
- To support items reported on tax returns

Of these six reasons, five are related to the preparation and factual verification of your tax return. The IRS will not be satisfied with unsupported allegations of income and expenses. Documentation should support everything you allege on your tax return.

Download *Publication 583, Starting a Business and Keeping Records* from the IRS website (**www.irs.gov/pub/irs-pdf/p583.pdf**). Print this document, and refer to it often during the startup phase of your recordkeeping.

An important benefit of keeping good records is that it prepares you for a potential audit by the IRS. An audit can be a stressful and frightening experience for a small business owner, but the anxiety associated with it can be reduced greatly by keeping detailed and organized records. During an audit, the IRS will challenge claims you made on your tax return. Most of the time, when the IRS challenges a claim, you will bear the burden of proving its accuracy. For example, suppose you claim a deduction for $1,000 related to a business expense for packaging materials and shipping costs. The IRS audits your return and challenges this expense. It is your responsibility to prove that those expenses actually were incurred. Unless you can present physical evidence of these expenses (receipts, checks, etc.), you have not carried your burden of proof, and the deduction will be disallowed. Obviously, keeping records of these transactions is crucial.

How does the IRS select individual taxpayers for audits?

The IRS procedure for selecting individuals for audit is a closely guarded secret. Though the current audit rate for individuals is only about 2 percent, certain factors can increase your chances of being audited. Several of these factors are relatively common characteristics of online sellers. Individuals who operate an Internet sales business increase their likelihood of being audited simply by being engaged in the activity. For example, large numbers of itemized deductions, home office deductions, self-employment, and the possible existence of unreported taxable income are all red flags for the IRS. Therefore, it is especially important for online sellers to keep detailed and organized records.

As discussed in Chapter 1, recordkeeping is also a key factor in determining whether your Internet sales activities are considered a hobby or a business. The more detailed and organized your records are, the more likely your activities will be considered a business and not a hobby. As a business, you will be entitled to numerous deductions when filing your taxes. Keep records in a manner that supports your claim that your online sales activities are a business.

Type of Information to Record

When you first start your online sales business, the thought of keeping records might seem overwhelming. What records should I keep? Where do I store all of my records? How should they be organized? How long should I keep my records? The law does not require that you keep your records in any specific manner. Though this gives you greater flexibility, it presents the daunting task of figuring out what information is relevant and how it should be documented.

Several components make up a recordkeeping system. You will need to keep written records of all the money that comes in and goes out of your business. This can be done with ledger books, spreadsheets, or with one of the accounting software systems described below. In addition, there are statements from banks, credit cards, and online marketplaces that contain information about the transactions occurring in each of them. Every transaction is supported by documents, such as receipts, invoices, and packing slips. All of this information must be kept filed and organized so you can refer to it when needed. At first, your recordkeeping system might be simple, but as your business expands into new products and activities, it can become more complex.

This section is an overview of the types of records you will need to keep and the types of information that should be included in each account. Although the process of setting up your recordkeeping system seems tedious, starting off on the right foot will save you time and money in the long run and make it easy to prepare your tax returns at the end of each year.

Four types of information should be found in your business records:

- Gross receipts
- Purchases
- Expenses
- Assets

Each of these items will be a separate account in your records. Keep each of these accounts independently, and include all the necessary information in each one. This section describes the types of information included in each account and the kinds of statements or documentation that should be kept for each entry. Distinguish among each of your accounts, and place a specific cost or item of income in the right category. If you are able to do this, you are well on your way to setting up an effective bookkeeping system.

Publication 583: Starting a Business and Keeping Records

IRS *Publication 583* provides a detailed account of the importance of keeping records and gives recommendations on how these records should be kept. Publication 583 can be found at **www.irs.gov/pub/irs-pdf/p583.pdf**.

Gross receipts

Gross receipts are the total amounts of money you receive from all sources before accounting for expenses and losses. This includes the total amount a buyer pays for the items you sell. All money received must be recorded as income, regardless of whether you get to keep it or not. All the costs you pay from the money you receive, such as shipping costs and the money you spend to buy the items you sell, will be recorded in the purchases or expenses accounts. The amount of your gross receipts is corroborated by documents, such as bank deposit slips, receipt books, invoices, bank statements, and IRS 1099 forms reporting payments made to contract workers.

The sales report function of an online sales marketplace can help keep track of gross receipts by providing an overview of all the activity in your account during a given period. Review your sales reports on a monthly basis, and reconcile them with your records, so you will have an accurate figure for your gross receipts at the end of the tax year.

As an example, look at the income categories for an eBay seller. EBay has three pricing models: sellers can sell the item to the highest bidder in an auction, for a fixed "Buy It Now" price if the buyer does not want to participate in an auction, or for a fixed price without an auction. The gross receipts for a typical eBay seller would include:

- Total eBay income (final bid amounts, "Buy It Now" amounts, and fixed-price amounts)

- Total eBay relist refunds (If a buyer does not submit payment, or you cancel a transaction, or end a listing early, and then relist the item and sell it, eBay might refund you the fee for the first listing.)

- Shipping costs charged to buyers

- Actual cost of shipping and handling

- Shipping and handling fees charged to the buyer that exceed actual cost of shipping and handling (EBay automatically calculates shipping costs and charges each buyer. Some items cost less to ship than the shipping charge paid by the buyer.)

- All sales tax collected

- Bank interest on your business account

Records for auction sites such as eBay are more complex because the final selling price is decided by bidders and will be different for every item. Sites where items sell for fixed prices are simpler, but you might still have to keep track of a variety of fees charged for enhanced listings, additional photos, and so on. For example, a spreadsheet for items sold on Amazon might list:

- Total amount received from Amazon

- Sale price of the item

- Amount charged by Amazon for shipping

- Actual cost of shipping

- Shipping and handling fees charged to the buyer that exceed the actual cost of shipping and handling.

- Amazon referral fee of 6 to 25 percent of the sale price (depends on the category of merchandise)

- Amazon variable closing fee (based on the type of merchandise and weight of the item)

- Amazon $0.99 fixed closing fee

- All sales tax collected

- Bank interest on your business account

It might seem strange to treat a relist refund as income, but in accounting terms, it is income because it is a credit given to you. The same is true of the shipping fees paid by the buyer. They are income because they were paid to you, even though you will not keep the money.

Purchases

The **purchases account** includes any item you buy for your business that you plan to resell to customers. For sellers who produce or manufacture the goods they sell online, the purchases account also includes the cost of any raw materials bought to create the goods sold to customers. This information should show a description of each item and the amount paid

for it. Examples of documents that include this kind of information are canceled checks, credit card sales slips, store receipts, and invoices.

Imagine for a moment that you sell used books through an eBay account, and you acquire most of the books that you sell from garage or estate sales. Every time you purchase books, you will need to get a receipt from the seller including the date of the sale, the name of the seller, a description of the books purchased, and the price paid. Ideally, you would pay with a credit card or check so that either the credit card receipt or the canceled check can serve as further documentation of the sale. Most garage sales are cash-only, however, so obtaining a receipt is particularly important. File any receipts or canceled checks related to the purchase, and make a corresponding entry in your purchases account to reflect the purchase of the item.

Expenses

Expenses are the costs you incur in carrying on your online sales business. Examples of common expenses for online sales businesses include shipping costs, packaging materials, office equipment, office supplies, and utility bills. It is important to distinguish expenses from purchases. The items you are selling and the supplies used to make any items sold are purchases, not expenses. Documents supporting expenses should show the amount of the expense and enough information about the expense to identify it. Examples of documents that show expenses are canceled checks, credit card sales slips, invoices, and receipts.

Your business expenses will vary, depending on the type of online marketplace you use, the fees it charges, and the way you handle payment and shipping. Below is a list of the typical expenses for someone selling on eBay. EBay has an arrangement with the U.S. Post Office so that the postage for shipping an item is calculated as part of the final charge to the buyer on eBay, and the seller can then purchase that postage online through PayPal.

- EBay listing fees (basic fees and fees for additional options)

- EBay final value fees (the commission or fee paid to eBay based on the total amount of each sale)

- Fees to PayPal (not including amounts paid to PayPal for postage purchased through eBay)

- Losses from fees on auctions that did not sell

- Money paid to shipping companies (including actual postage purchased through PayPal)

- Cost of shipping materials

- Office supplies

- Larger purchases (equipment, office furniture, software upgrades)

- Accounting or attorney's fees

- Sales tax forwarded to the state (if it is not automatically deducted during the sale)

- Your time/labor (This cannot be claimed as a business expenses for tax purposes)

- Bank fees on your business account (service charges, overdraft fees)

Expenses for selling items on Amazon might include:

- Amazon referral fee of 6 to 25 percent of the sale price

- Amazon variable closing fee

- Amazon $0.99 fixed closing fee

- Losses from listing fees on items that did not sell

- Money paid to shipping companies

- Cost of shipping materials

- Office supplies

- Larger purchases (equipment, office furniture, software upgrades)

- Accounting or attorney's fees

- Sales tax forwarded to the state (if it is not automatically deducted during the sale)

- Your time/labor (This cannot be claimed as a business expenses for tax purposes)

- Bank fees on your business account (service charges, overdraft fees)

Your list of expenses can be as detailed as you wish to make it. The best records reflect every aspect of the business, regardless of how insignificant it seems. For example, if you only record "expenses" in general without breaking them up into categories, how would you know when you are spending an excessive amount on office supplies every month? Wasteful spending is easier to spot when you can see in real numbers what you spend on each category every month. You might want to track the different fees charged by your online marketplace, such as regular listing fees and fees for additional features and services (such as extra photos) separately. This level of detail is not necessary for tax purposes, but it will help you evaluate your business practices over time. For example, if you discover that listings with extra photos sell the first time around and do not need to be relisted, you might decide extra photos are worth the higher fees. On the other hand, you might discover that having extra photos makes no difference at all to how quickly an item sells and is not worth the extra expense.

Assets

The **assets account** includes property that you own or rent to carry on your business. Common examples are rented office space, machinery used to make the items you sell, and large office equipment, such as computers. Depending on the nature of your sales, you might not use this type of account at all.

A different account must be maintained for each one of these categories. One account tracks only expenses, one account tracks only purchases, one account tracks only gross receipts, and one account tracks only assets.

Examples of Supporting Documentation

All of your income and expense records should reflect information found on documents such as sales receipts, invoices, and statements from your online marketplace and your bank. These documents should be organized and filed so you can access them when you need to.

Canceled check

A canceled check is one of the best sources of information for your record-keeping system, and much of the information that needs to be included in your records can be found on it, such as the payee, amount, check number, date, and even the purpose. Unfortunately, it can be difficult to maintain copies of canceled checks. Most banks no longer send you paper copies of canceled checks, and scanned images of them are made available online for only a few months. Many purchases are now made using debit cards rather than checks. Each month, review your bank statement online, and save copies of the images of canceled checks on your computer.

Electronic funds transfer

You might use an electronic funds transfer service such as PayPal to receive money and pay for purchases. If you use this method, note the amount that was transferred, the payee's name, and the date the transfer was posted to your business's bank account. You will be able to download and print reports directly from the website of the electronic funds transfer service.

Credit cards and debit cards

If you use a credit card or debit card to pay for purchases, your monthly bank statement or credit card statement is evidence of your transactions. Your records should include the amount that was charged, the payee's name, the date of transaction, and its purpose.

A bank or credit card statement alone might not be enough evidence that a particular transaction qualifies as a purchase or business expense. This warning is posted on the IRS website: "Proof of payment of an amount, by itself, does not establish you are entitled to a tax deduction. You should also keep other documents, such as credit card sales slips and invoices, to show that you also incurred the cost."

Business checking account and credit card

One of the first things to do when you set up your online sales business is to open a dedicated business checking account. This account should be separate from your personal checking account and be used for only those matters related to your online sales. All receipts related to your sales should be deposited into this account, and all expenses associated with selling items through online marketplaces should be paid out of this account. When this checking account is used purely for matters related to your online business, the records relating to that account can serve as supporting documentation for any expenses paid through that account. Similarly, you might consider opening a credit card account to be used only for business-related purposes. The records from this account can serve a function similar to those of the checking account.

How Long to Keep Records

Typically, the IRS has three years from the date the return is due to initiate an audit. This means you should keep all records related to a specific year's tax return for at least three years. In certain circumstances, the IRS is allowed six years from the date the return is due to initiate an audit. One of these circumstances is when the IRS determines that the amount of income you omitted from your return was more than 25 percent of the amount of income you reported. This exception to the normal three-year rule is referred to as a **substantial understatement of income exception**. The IRS is given extra time to audit a return with a substantial understatement of income because Congress assumed it would take the IRS longer to discover the substantial understatement than other problems with a taxpayer's return, such as discrepancy between a taxpayer's W-2 and 1040.

It is recommended that you keep all supporting documents for six years. Once you have compiled the records for a year and used them to prepare your tax return, you should retain these records in a centralized place for six years after the due date of the return. Consider keeping an electronic and a hard copy of your records. If you find it too onerous to maintain hard copies because of the number of records, consider backing up your records to an external hard drive or online data storage site, such as Mozy® (**http://mozy.com**) or SugarSync (**www.sugarsync.com**). SugarSync offers five GB of free storage, and Mozy charges $3.95 plus $.50 per GB per month.

In addition to the records used to prepare your tax return, you also should keep copies of your filed tax returns. Past returns can help you prepare future returns and provide valuable information if you need to file an amended return.

Finally, ask yourself a few common sense questions before ultimately deciding to send the documents to the shredder:

- Are the documents still relevant?

- Will keeping them help me serve some purpose in the future?

- If I throw them out, will it cause problems later?

If you answer these questions and find that there is no other reason to retain certain records, you can confidently dispose of them after six years.

Organizing Receipts

Receipts are the individual records for each of the expenditures associated with running your online business. Keeping your business's receipts is an important element of proper bookkeeping because they contain the raw data upon which your accounts and books are based. The information on a receipt should include the items purchased, the date of purchase, the price of each item, the total price (including taxes and shipping, if applicable), the terms of the purchase, and who bought the item.

Though it seems like a large amount of paper, you need to retain receipts for most purchases you make and expenses you pay throughout the year. These receipts serve two functions. First, they provide you with the relevant information for many of the deductions discussed in later chapters. Second, they are evidence you actually incurred the expenses you are claiming as deductions on your tax return. Even if you could remember how much you spent throughout the year without the receipts,

during an audit the IRS will ask to see physical proof that those expenditures actually were made. Therefore, it is necessary to have some method of storing and filing the receipts for expenses and purchases made throughout the year. You can use file folders, a shoe box, or digital storage; any method that stores the documents in an easily accessible manner is fine. Receipts that are related to the same tax year should be filed together, and receipts that are related to the same type of expenditure (expense or purchase) should be grouped together within a specific year. It is also helpful to group receipts according to the category of expense or purchase so you do not have to sort them out at the end of the financial year.

Creating a Filing System

A basic filing cabinet is all you will need to store your paper trail, at least for now. Set up files in a manner that makes sense to you and is not too complicated or time consuming. Here is a suggested list of file folders for an Internet sales business:

- Invoices from the online marketplace, typically sent electronically every month or printed out from the site

- PayPal statements, which can be printed out from the PayPal site

- Individual summaries of each PayPal transaction stapled to any other documentation for that particular auction or sale, such as a delivery confirmation receipt or tracking numbers. The monthly statements do not specify what each transaction was for.

- Business bank account statements, with an envelope to put all deposit slips and other documentation for that month

- Receipts for all inventory purchases

- Receipts for all office or business supplies (shipping supplies, printer paper, etc.)

- Receipts for all shipping, including delivery confirmation receipts and insurance documents. If you purchase shipping through PayPal or online from the U.S. Postal Service (**www.usps.com**), FedEx (**www.fedex.com**), or another shipping company, much of this information can be accessed by printing off the transaction record.

At the end of every month, staple, clip, or place in envelopes all the appropriate items from each folder together so they will not get mixed up with the next month's items as you place them in the file. If you are careful to save and print out all supporting documentation, you should have all the information you will need for your end-of-year tax filing.

Bookkeeping

Bookkeeping refers the more technical aspects of the recordkeeping process, such as entering data and calculations into a chart or spreadsheet. There are several considerations when you set up the bookkeeping for your business. You must decide who will be keeping your books, the basic techniques involved for different accounts, how to set up your books, and finally, how to keep your books updated.

Bookkeeping can be done on paper or with computer software. An accountant can help you set up a chart of accounts based on the list of income and expenses you made earlier, with category titles and/or a numbering system (for ease of entering transactions). Accounting software is more efficient when you input all the data necessary for proper reporting and tracking of income and expenses.

Accounting software programs

Accounting software packages offer complete accounting systems that do just about everything: keep track of income, expenses, and sales tax; create invoices; do your payroll; process credit card transactions; import data from your bank statements and online shopping carts; print checks; produce instant customized reports; and create budgets, forecasts, and business plans.

One of the most widely used packages, known for its versatility and ease of use, is QuickBooks™ financial software. The basic version of this program, QuickBooks Pro, sells for less than $230 at office supply retailers. An online version is available starting at $10 per month. QuickBooks Pro can print checks, pay bills, keep track of your expenses, and track sales, sales tax, and customer payments. QuickBooks' Premier Edition is a complete accounting system that sells for approximately $400. QuickBooks can be purchased online directly from the QuickBooks website at **www.quickbooks.intuit.com** or other sites such as Amazon.com (**www.amazon.com**). Each version of QuickBooks comes with an introductory course on you how to use your new software correctly.

Another popular accounting package is Sage Peachtree Complete Accounting 2011 (**www.peachtree.com**), which sells for about $300 and offers more inventory options than QuickBooks. Although the setup is a little complicated, it is easy to use once you have it up and running.

You can find in-depth reviews of the top ten small business accounting software packages at Top Ten Reviews™ (**http://accounting-software-review.toptenreviews.com**).

All of these software packages have live-support options and add-ons, such as credit-card processing services for an additional cost. They can be customized to fit your business needs. Have an accountant or someone who knows the program help you set it up so it does exactly what you need it to do. Once the program is set up, all you have to do is enter your records on a regular basis.

Accounting software is a business expense

If you decide to invest in any recordkeeping software, remember to keep track of all receipts and note the cost of the software as an expense in your records. The cost associated with your software may be a deductible business expense.

If you are not ready to invest in accounting software, you can track expenses is with a spreadsheet program such as Microsoft® Excel, part of the Microsoft Office suite. There is a simple spreadsheet program in the free Microsoft Works that comes installed on most personal computers. Basic spreadsheets are not difficult to set up once you have some knowledge of how they work. Free online tutorials at websites such as Microsoft.com (**http://office. microsoft.com/en-us/excel-help**) and Baycon Group (**www.baycon group.com/el0.htm**) will teach you how to work with spreadsheets.

If you do not yet have Excel, accounting software, an accountant, or the knowledge to put the software to work for you, do not delay recording details of your auction transactions. Begin immediately. Set up your file folders, and keep every piece of documentation. You can always analyze day-to-day expenses and income the old-fashioned way with a ledger book, a bound set of blank sheets with preprinted grids of rows and columns purchased from an office supply store.

Sales spreadsheet

There are a number of ways to set up a ledger or a spreadsheet, depending on what you wish to track. Label each column across the top of your spreadsheet or ledger with a heading, and then enter the information for each transaction across one of the rows beneath. Begin a new page for every month. Below is an example of the column headings you might use to track sales on eBay. If you are using a spreadsheet on your computer, you can format expense columns so the figures are enclosed in parentheses or colored red to show that they are being subtracted from income.

Sample column headings for an eBay seller

COLUMN	TITLE	EXPLANATION
A	Inventory number	A unique number that you assign to each item that you sell
B	Auction start/end	Beginning and end dates of online auction
C	Relisted Item Y/N	Y means the item did not sell the first time and was relisted. The original listing fee would be recorded as a loss in the month that the item did not sell, but if the same item is listed again within 90 days and sells, eBay might refund the original listing fee. A "Y" in this column tells you to be on the lookout for a refund, which should be recorded in Column N.
D	Acquisition cost	This is the total cost incurred in obtaining or producing/making this item, including labor and materials if you made it yourself. Keep all receipts and records to completely support this amount.
E	EBay listing fee	The basic, flat fee paid to eBay to list this product. This does not include extra services, enhancements, or charges.
F	EBay listing charges	Fees for optional services for this auction or sale on eBay. Each service is listed individually with a code number followed by the amount of the additional fee.
G	Final value fee	This is the incremental fee charged by eBay based on the sales price of the item. There will be a "0" in this column if the item did not sell.

COLUMN	TITLE	EXPLANATION
H	PayPal fee	The fee charged by PayPal to process this transaction — currently 1.9% to 2.9% + $0.30. This does not include amounts paid to PayPal to buy postage.
I	Postage	Cost of shipping the item to the buyer, including insurance, delivery confirmation, and express shipping
J	Sales tax	Amount of sales tax you will report and pay for this sale
K	Total out	The items in columns D to J are all expenses, so the amounts are in parentheses, which means they are "subtracted" from the income columns. The total of all the expense columns goes here.
L	Gross sold price	The total amount the item sold for, not including sales tax, or shipping and handling fees and charges
M	Total shipping and handling charged	The total amount paid by the buyer for shipping and handling. It may be more than Column I if a shipping and handling charge was included in the price, or if eBay automatically calculated shipping charges.
N	Relisted refund amount	Refund of original listing fee for an item that was relisted on eBay and sold with 90 days. EBay will notify you if you are eligible for this refund.
O	Sales tax	Amount charged as sales tax, if you will be filing and paying sales tax. If sales tax is automatically paid by eBay, this column will be "0".
P	Total in	Add the amounts in columns L to O. This is the gross income from the sale.
Q	Net profit	Subtract the amount in Column K from the amount in Column P. This is the profit you have made on the sale.

The spreadsheet above shows you how much profit you are making on each sale, how much profit you are making by overcharging for shipping and handling, and how much you are paying for extra services and listing options. By analyzing the information in this spreadsheet, you could decide whether to increase or lower the markup on your acquisition cost for each item, whether you are charging enough for shipping and handling, and whether enhanced listing options are worth the extra expense.

This ledger shows your income from eBay sales. If you are using multiple online marketplaces, you might keep a separate ledger sheet for each one or modify this one to accommodate all of your sales channels. For example, you could add a column to show which online marketplace was used to list each item and columns for other types of fees or charges.

Inventory spreadsheet

The sales ledger above shows all of your income from online sales, as well as the amounts of your purchases (in the acquisition cost column), and some of your business expenses (listing fees and shipping). You will need another ledger or spreadsheet to keep track of your inventory. You cannot price your items to make a profit if you do not know how much you spent to acquire them.

The columns in your inventory ledger should include the source of each item in the inventory, date purchased, how much you paid for it, cost of having it shipped to you and repairs (if any), date sold, and how much you sold it for. If you are selling many unique items, such as antique toys or stamps, add more columns. You could have columns for receipt or transaction numbers, buyer's e-mail addresses and contact information, date when an item has been returned, shipping costs, and insurance. If a customer contacts you with a complaint, you will be able to look up all the information about his or her order in one place. You also can build up a list of clients who might be interested in buying similar items in the future.

When you acquire inventory at estate sales, flea markets, or garage sales, you probably will not be provided with a receipt for your records. In this case, pull out your little spiral notebook (kept in your car for tracking mileage), and write a receipt for yourself. When you return home, you can accurately record your acquisition costs of the items. When you purchase numerous items at one sale, you will quickly forget how much you paid for each and could end up asking too little for an item later. If you end up taking a loss on an item purchased secondhand, you will need some documentation of what you paid for it in order to subtract it from your income for the month. Keep in mind that during an audit, the IRS might question the validity of these makeshift receipts, so try to be as thorough as possible.

Keeping accurate records of what you paid for each item will give you a true picture of your business.

If you are manufacturing your product using a variety of supplies, equipment, and materials, you might need a separate ledger to keep track of these expenses and calculate the acquisition cost of each item. Do not forget to include the cost of utilities if you are operating electrical equipment or using water, labor if you employ any workers to help you, and transportation and shipping costs for your raw materials.

Some accounting software packages have inventory management components that allow you to enter information about your items and automatically tie it in with sales data. For example, when you mark an item as sold in the income account, the inventory record for that item will be updated immediately with information about the sale. If you are familiar with Excel, you can link your spreadsheets so that information you enter into one is updated in another.

Business expenses

Use another ledger sheet, spreadsheet, or bookkeeping account to keep track of business expenses. Earlier in the chapter, you learned that products you buy for resale are recorded in the purchase account, while everything else you buy for your business is recorded in the expense account. Some of the data from your sales ledger belongs in the purchase account and some in the expense account. Your acquisition cost for each item you sell is recorded as a purchase. The other costs associated with your online marketplace sales, such as listing fees, upgrades, shipping and postage, and packaging materials, are considered business expenses. Other expenses such as office supplies and furnishings, computer accessories, domain name registrations, and even mileage for a vehicle used for business purposes are recorded in the expense account. If your online sales activities are a business and not a hobby, these expenses can be deducted from your taxable income on your tax return. *Deductions will be discussed in more detail in Chapter 4.*

Online Marketplace Tools

In addition to monthly statements and sales reports, most online marketplaces provide tools to help sellers organize their records. For example, eBay provides My eBay; Selling Manager and Selling Manager Pro; Blackthorne Basic and Blackthorne Pro; File Exchange; Sales Reports and Sales Reports Plus; and eBay marketplace research. Sellers on Etsy.com (**www.etsy.com/ apps/shop_tools**) can choose from a variety of third-party applications (apps) to enhance their sales and analyze their market activity. These tools can help you keep track of listing fees, shipping costs, and sale prices, as well as provide detailed information about the performance of your listing.

EBay tools

My eBay

My eBay provides an overview of all your sales activity in one place. It provides information about current listings, buyers, and other details related to the items you are selling. You can track your items, leave feedback, and receive payments through this section. One of the most useful functions of My eBay is its ability to kept track of total sales over the past 60 days. When managed correctly, this function can give you a total picture of your yearly sales. Sellers should print off the account overview My eBay generates every month.

Selling Manager

The Selling Manager allows you to manage your sales and keep inventory more easily. You can leave and receive feedback, communicate with your clients, and create and send invoices and shipping labels. Your sales history can be exported to a spreadsheet program such as Excel, which will help you keep better records with less work. Selling Manager Pro, an upgrade that costs $15.99 a month, creates monthly profit and loss reports and compares the success ratios for the products you sell.

Sales Reports

The Sales Reports feature is free to all sellers and provides two different categories of basic information about your eBay sales at the end of each month. The Sales Summary is a snapshot of your sales for the month. The Fees Summary provides information about your net fees for eBay and PayPal.

The Sales Reports function archives your old Sales Reports for up to six months. Because eBay retains this information for only six months, print out each month's Sales Reports and retain it for your records. Sales Reports Plus allows you to separate your reports into individual categories and evaluate the performance of your items to determine which categories are outperforming others.

Accounting Assistant

Accounting Assistant allows you automatically to transfer information about your sales, including sales price and fees, directly into QuickBooks. Accounting Assistant also can be used to transfer your PayPal fee information directly from PayPal to QuickBooks.

PayPal

PayPal is a separate company but is owned by the same company that owns eBay. PayPal reports give you a complete record of all your purchases and payments and lets you print out monthly statements.

Evidence of a business

As mentioned in Chapter 1, sellers engaged in a business activity often get better tax treatment than those engaged in a hobby activity. Using the Sales Reports Plus category functions to monitor your sales and critically evaluate the performance of each category to make your business more profitable indicates you are engaged in a business activity rather than a hobby.

Updating Your Books

Get into the habit of keeping records meticulously. Every time you incur a cost related to your online sales, remember to keep a record of that cost and note it in the appropriate account. Did you stop by the office supply store today to pick up extra packaging tape? Keep your receipt, and be sure to add an entry for this cost to your expense account. Did you visit a couple of garage sales last weekend to buy some items to resell? Make sure you get a receipt from the seller and add an entry for this cost to your purchase account.

Recording and retaining every receipt for every cost associated with your online sales is the only way to ensure you can take advantage of all available tax deductions. Without accurate records of how much you spend on what, you never will be able to correctly calculate the amount of tax you owe. In the end, failing to keep detailed records can cost you money by depriving you of important deductions.

How and when you update your books depends on what kind of new information you have, how often you receive it, and where you will record it. Gross receipts, expenses, purchases, and assets are each a separate account in your records. Keep in mind which account you are updating and what kind of new information should trigger an update.

Daily updates

Ideally, every time you incur an expense, you should update your books. It is easy to get absorbed in the daily tasks associated with listing and selling online, but a fresh memory is your best ally when it comes to documenting your finances. When you go out to buy packaging supplies, the first thing you should do when you get back to your office or computer is make a record of this in your expense account and file the receipt that corresponds with that expense. There will be numerous daily expenses, especially in the early stages of your business, and remembering all of them can be difficult if you do not diligently record them as soon as you incur them. The only way to ensure your records accurately reflect your expenses is to keep track meticulously of every penny you spend. Get in the habit of recording an expense and filing its receipt as soon as it is incurred. The same is true of costs associated with purchases and assets. Any time you incur a cost related to a purchase of a new asset for your business, you should file the receipt and record the cost in the appropriate account.

An online business with a high sales volume of unique items might incur multiple expenses every day, while someone who is processing orders for a product that is drop-shipped could require only an occasional ream of printer paper or box of pens. Not everyone has the inclination to record every purchase right away. If you only incur an occasional expense, or if you do not have time for daily updates, bundle all the receipts for your expenses in one envelope so they do not get lost, and file them away each month so you or your accountant can sort them out at tax time.

Accounting software allows you to update your records automatically by importing information directly from online bank statements, credit card statements, PayPal statements, and sales activity reports from your online marketplaces. If you make all of your purchases with a debit card or credit card, you will be able to run automatic updates periodically that populate (enter data) your account spreadsheets with information about each expense. These updates takes some time at first because you have to tell the software where some of the credit card charges should be recorded, but once you have set up your system, automatic updates take only a few minutes. Anything you buy with cash will not be included in these updates, so you will have to record those expenses manually and be careful to file the receipts. A receipt will be the only evidence to document that expense.

How often you need to update your records also depends on the volume of activity in your online sales business. You should be aware of how much you are spending so you can control your costs. If your business is active, up-to-date records will help you identify potential problems before they rob you of your profits.

Monthly updates

Your gross receipts account can be updated at the end of each month. The monthly sales report from your online marketplace summarizes your sales and includes the total amount of sales for the month. At the end of every month, save and print your sales report. Record the total sales amount for the month in your gross receipts account, and keep a copy of the sales report in your records. It is important to save a copy of your sales report at the end of each month on your computer, a flash drive, or an online data storage account because most online marketplaces only retain sales report for six months.

Your sales report also will contain the total amount of fees incurred during the month. This information should be recorded as an expense at the end of each month.

The end of the month is also a good time to save copies of all new invoices sent to buyers. These invoices will serve as a record of the individual price paid for each item.

Annual updates

If you are diligent about updating your records daily and monthly, there will be little updating required at the end of the tax year. The only additional information that will need to be added to the records for a given year is information related to your tax returns. Once you fill out your tax return, make copies of it, and place these copies with the records for that year. These combined records should be stored together for at least six years. These documents can provide a wealth of information about your online sales business and will be essential if the IRS audits you.

Reconciling your Account Statements

Reconcile your business bank account statement with your records each month. Confirm that the amounts on the bank statement for each transaction are the same as the amounts in your records. If you are using accounting software, then you can import or link to your bank statement and run an automatic reconciliation that will list any abnormalities or missing amounts in a Discrepancy Report. You also can import or copy and paste your bank statement to a spreadsheet and do a reconciliation using Microsoft Excel. Bank reconciliation templates can be found on the Microsoft Office website (**http://office.microsoft.com/en-us/templates#**). To do a manual reconciliation, compare a printed copy of your bank statement to the amounts in your records, and put a checkmark next to each amount as you confirm it. Investigate missing or incorrect amounts to find errors.

Similarly, compare your records with PayPal statements and sales reports from your online marketplace. You can download both online marketplace and PayPal statements and save them on your computer or import them into software, including Excel and most accounting systems. Though electronic statements are typically accurate, comparing your invoices with your monthly spreadsheet, log sheet, or accounting program will ensure you did not overlook something.

When you have finished, mark invoices and bank statements as "reconciled" before filing, so you do not forget and repeat the work later on.

Protecting your Business Records

While you are setting up your recordkeeping system, give some thought to ensuring the safety of your business records. Your office should include a filing cabinet where you can organize and store your documents in one place. If you are setting up shop in a room in your home, consider installing a door with a lock to prevent a well-meaning spouse or family member from messing up a pile of receipts or accidentally throwing away an important paper. A locked door will keep curious pets, children, or visitors from inadvertently causing chaos.

Another potential hazard is a house fire. If all your data is up-to-date and stored safely (in a fireproof safe or off-site), you will have everything you need to file accurate insurance claims and get back to work quickly, and you will still be able to file your taxes on time. Properly installed smoke detectors and a sprinkler system are good investments.

Are you covered by insurance?

Check with your insurance company to see whether your homeowners or renters policy would cover business losses in case of a house fire or other natural disaster, break-in, or other malicious act by others. If you are not covered, your agent can amend your policy or sell you a different policy designed to cover your business.

Protection for your computer

Your computer and Internet connection are crucial to your Internet sales business — you use them to create and edit images, set up listings, do research, and communicate with customers. You must regularly monitor your e-mail and your sales account for incoming orders, manage incoming payments, print packing slips and shipping labels, and write letters and e-mails. In addition, you maintain all your financial records on your computer, including copies of electronic statements and scanned copies of receipts. If you experience even a few hours when you cannot connect to the Internet or use your computer, your business suffers. For this reason, you must protect your computer from computer viruses and electric power surges that could destroy your hard drive or make your computer unusable. Spend the extra money for high-end surge protectors, and get the best virus and firewall protection you can find.

Always have a backup power supply and a reliable Internet connection

Your business activities can be interrupted if a network failure disrupts Internet connections or if a computer system suddenly shuts down because of a power failure. You can purchase a backup power supply for your computer at an electronics or office supply store. Often, a backup power supply is combined with a powerful surge protector. You plug the power supply into an electrical outlet and then plug your computer and all its peripherals (such as monitors, speakers, and external hard drives) into the power supply. Contact your Internet service provider if you experience persistent Internet disconnections and ask them to help you resolve the problem. Always have a backup computer you can use to access the Internet if your computer is down for an extended period. You can go and do essential tasks at a neighbor or relative's house, a library, cyber café, or a coffee shop with Wi-Fi (wireless Internet).

All your accounting records, customer databases, and stored e-mail could be lost in a second if you do not have your system backed up regularly. You can find instructions for setting up regular backups of your computer system and data files on your computer manufacturer's website. An automatic backup saves copies of your files on a CD, DVD, flash drive, an external hard drive, and/or online. A number of companies, such as CrashPlan™ (**www.crashplan.com**), Carbonite® (**www.carbonite.com**), IDrive®

(**www.idrive.com**), charge from less than $5 to $10 per month to back up your business data on their servers. It is a good idea to keep a backup of your data online or at another physical location in case your office equipment is destroyed by fire, theft, or some other mishap. If you do not use an online backup, you can copy your data onto an additional flash drive or external hard drive from time to time and store it at another location.

Do not forget to save backup copies of your websites, e-mails, photos, graphics, and any other files that you might need for your business.

If you do not know enough about computers, a computer repair shop or the computer center in an electronics store can assist you in setting up virus protection and an appropriate backup system.

Cost of data storage is a business expense

If you choose to purchase storage space in the form of an external hard drive or from an online site, remember to keep a record of this cost and make a note of it under the expense heading of your records. This is a cost of carrying on your business and might be deductible when computing taxable income.

CHAPTER 3

Taxes That Affect Small Businesses

T his chapter highlights some aspects of small business taxes that apply to online sales businesses. It is important to understand how the tax code affects your business activities from the beginning. Do not wait until you are filling out your tax return to discover that you should have been making quarterly income tax payments or saving receipts for repairs done to your home. Some of the tax breaks described in this book require advance planning. Once you have filed your taxes for your first year of business, you will have a better understanding of what is involved. In the meantime, this chapter can help you prepare well in advance so when it is time to do your taxes, you will have all the necessary information on hand, and the process will be streamlined.

Levels of Taxation

All business owners must pay taxes to the U.S. government under the federal system. In addition, depending on state and local laws, a business might be required to pay taxes on the state and local levels. Often, income tax must be paid on all three levels. State and local requirements differ from federal tax laws; learn how and when you are expected to file and pay taxes. In addition to income tax, states and local regions expect you to collect and pay sales tax, and might charge a business tax or a business license fee. To know what taxes you are required to pay, you must determine the geographical location where your business has "nexus" — a physical presence.

Ignorance of state and local tax requirements has negative consequences beyond any penalties you might have to pay. Many of the taxes paid on local and state levels are deductible from the taxable income on which your federal income tax is based. These include state and local income taxes, real estate taxes, income taxes paid to a foreign government, and sales or excise taxes on the purchase of a new vehicle. Business licenses and other fees may be deductible as business expenses. If you are unaware of the various taxes you are paying and the deductions that might be available to you, you might miss out on significant opportunities to reduce your taxable income.

Types of Taxes

The types of taxes most likely to affect you are sales tax, use tax, payroll tax, self-employment tax, and federal and state income tax. A few other taxes might be important to you if you have employees or if you are dealing in merchandise such as motor vehicles or wines.

Sales tax

Sales taxes are paid to state and sometimes local governments. Most states' sales tax rates are 6 percent to 8 percent, but some are higher or lower. For example, Alaska has only a 1.05 percent sales tax rate while Tennessee's rate is 9.4 percent. Sales tax is paid only on retail purchases, not on the purchase of wholesale items for resale. *Chapter 10 discusses sales tax.*

Use tax

States that charge sales tax also impose a use tax when you purchase an item for your own use and do not pay sales tax on it. For example, if you buy a computer for your office in another state and bring it back into your state, you will be expected to pay a use tax. Use tax also applies when you purchase used items, such as furniture or an old car, from a classified ad or a garage sale from someone who is not authorized to collect sales tax. Use tax applies to items you buy online without paying state sales tax. Some states only require businesses to pay use tax, while others require it of private individuals. Some states give you credit for sales tax charged by another state. Items such as food and prescription medications typically are exempt from use tax. You are not required to pay a use tax on items you will resell on an online marketplace because you will be charging sales tax on those sales.

Individuals ordinarily report and pay use tax with their state income tax returns. An Individual Sales and Use Tax Return might be required for a large transaction, such as used vehicle purchases. Businesses may have to file a Business Sales and Use Tax Return with the state taxing authority.

Become familiar with the use tax laws of your state. You can find out if your state charges a use tax by examining your state income tax form for a section titled "Use Tax" or by reading the tax information on your state's official website.

Payroll tax

If your business is structured as a corporation, you are required to set up a payroll for any employees that work for the business, including yourself. You must withhold federal income tax, Social Security tax, and Medicare tax from employees' paychecks and report wages and taxes on IRS Form 941 Employer's QUARTERLY Federal Tax Return (**www.irs.gov/pub/irs-pdf/f941.pdf**). If your monthly payroll taxes exceed $2,500, you will have to make a payment every month. Your bank will send payments to the IRS through the Electronic Federal Tax Payment System (EFTPS). *Chapter 6 discusses payroll taxes.*

Unemployment insurance and worker's compensation

Regardless of the size of your business, if you have employees you must pay for federal and state unemployment insurance (FUTA and SUTA). If something happens to your business, unemployment insurance provides financial support to your employees until they find new jobs. On the federal level, you only will be required to pay once a year. Most states' payment schedules require you to pay these taxes monthly. In some states, self-employed individuals can pay into an unemployment program to protect themselves if they lose their income.

Worker's compensation must be bought through an independent insurance agency, not the government. These taxes are paid on the state level, so you should be aware of your state's requirements.

Self-employment tax: Social Security and Medicare

If your business brings in an annual income of more than $400, you are required to pay self-employment taxes. When you work for an employer, the employer pays half of your Social Security and Medicare taxes, and you pay the other half out of your paycheck. When you are self-employed, you must pay the entire amount yourself. Self Employment Tax allows you to receive retirement benefits, disability benefits, survivor benefits, and hospital insurance (Medicare) benefits. You must have a Social Security number to pay self-employment tax. The current Social Security premium is 12.4 percent of your total, or gross, pay. (There is a temporary reduction of 2 percent in 2011 only). If your business is structured as a corporation, half of this amount comes from your personal earnings while your corporation pays the other half. Your Social Security maximum payment cannot exceed $6,621.60 because only your initial $106,800 in earnings is eligible.

The premium for Medicare is currently 2.9 percent of your total earnings with half coming from your corporation and half from yourself. Unlike Social Security, Medicare has no income limits.

Together, self-employment taxes amount to 15.3 percent of your total income up to $106,800 and 2.9 percent of your income above that.

Personal income tax

You are required to file an income tax return to report the income from your online sales business. Personal income taxes are filed using *Form 1040*, with your *Schedule C: Profit or Loss from Business* (**www.irs.gov/pub/irs-pdf/i1040sc.pdf**) attached to it. You must list your net profit or loss for each business you are operating. Income tax forms are due "by the 15th day of the 4th month after the end of your fiscal year," but you can fill out *Form 4868* to receive an extension.

Quarterly estimated tax

If you anticipate that you will owe more than $1,000 in income taxes for the year, you must file and pay quarterly income tax returns. Instead of paying once on April 15, you must make four payments due on January 15, April 15, June 15, and September 15 of each year. If your business is structured as a corporation and you are on the payroll, you can withhold income tax from your regular paycheck.

Other taxes

Business income tax

Corporations pay business income taxes on their income. Corporations are taxed at a higher rate than individuals. Business taxes are paid yearly rather than monthly or quarterly. In some cases, business income taxes are paid on the state as well as the federal level; so check the requirements for your state.

Property tax

If you own land or a house (known as real property), you will be required to pay local property taxes. Some states and localities also impose taxes on personal property, such as furniture, fixtures, office and industrial equipment, machinery, tools, supplies, inventory, and any other property not classified as real property. Check your state's website for the requirements in your state.

Inventory tax

Some states require businesses to pay inventory tax on various types of equipment, manufactured goods, and personal property, such as business furniture, fixtures, and equipment. Depending on your state, online sellers may be exempted from inventory tax, but you should be aware of your state's requirements. The following states charge inventory tax of some kind:

Alaska	Mississippi
Arkansas	Ohio
Georgia	Oklahoma
Indiana	Rhode Island
Kentucky	Texas
Louisiana	Vermont
Maryland	West Virginia
Massachusetts	

Business entity tax

Many states require businesses to pay a business entity tax (BET), a flat fee paid at the time your taxes are filed in April. The terms of the BET depend on the state in which your taxes are filed. For example, Connecticut charges corporations and LLCs an annual fee of $250. In Arkansas, LLCS must pay a minimum annual franchise tax of $150. In California, all LLCs pay $800 annually. Typically, corporations and limited liability companies (LLCs) pay BET. Check with your individual state's taxation office.

Excise tax

Excise taxes are paid when certain goods, such as alcohol, gasoline, and cigarettes, are purchased. They can also apply to certain activities that an individual may participate in, such as betting or highway usage by trucks. These taxes often are included in the price of the item. One of the most common excise taxes involves gasoline or fuel. You might have to pay or process excise taxes if you deal in:

- Alternative fuel
- Gas-guzzler automobiles (automobiles of a model type that do not meet certain standards for fuel economy)
- Sport fishing equipment (including fishing rods and fishing poles), fishing tackle boxes, bows, quivers, broadheads, points, and arrow shafts
- Ozone-depleting chemicals (ODCs)
- Alcohol
- Retail seller of certain heavy vehicles

Filing Excise taxes

Form 720 should be used for environmental products, air transportation taxes, fuel taxes, taxes on heavy trucks, trailers, and tractors, or manufacturer's taxes. *Form 2290* should be used for taxes on vehicles 55,000 pounds or more.

IRS Publication 334, Table 1-2: Which forms must I file?

TAX	FORM	DUE BY:
Income tax	1040 and Schedule C or C-EZ2	15th day of 4th month after end of tax year
Self-employment tax	Schedule SE File with Form 1040.	15th day of 4th month after end of tax year
Estimated tax	1040-ES	15th day of 4th, 6th, and 9th months
Social Security and Medicare taxes and income tax withholding	941 or 9445	April 30, July 31, October 31, and January 31 See Publication 15.
Providing information on Social Security and Medicare taxes and income tax withholding	W-2 (to employee) W-2 and W-3 (to the Social Security	January 31 Last day of February (March 31 if filing electronically)
Federal unemployment (FUTA) tax	940 or 940-EZ	April 30, July 31, October 31, and January 31, but only if the liability for unpaid tax is more than $500
Filing information returns for transactions with other persons	Form 1099-MISC or other Form 1099	Forms 1099 — to the recipient by payments to nonemployees and January 31 and to the IRS by transactions with other persons February 28 (March 31 if filing electronically)
Excise tax	Form 720, Quarterly Federal Excise Tax Return	April 30, July 31, October 31, and January 31
Sales tax	State and local forms or filing systems	Monthly
State and local income tax	State and local forms or filing systems	Typically the 15th day of 4th month after end of tax year

Tax ID Number (TIN)

You must include your federal Tax ID Number (TIN) on all tax documents. Chapter 1 emphasized the importance of getting a tax ID number before you begin operating your business. Most online sellers file taxes using their Social Security numbers (SSNs). If you do not have a SSN, you can get one by filling out a *Form SS-5*, which can be obtained at Social Security Administration offices or on the SSA website (**www.socialsecurity.gov**).

If you, a spouse, or a dependent included on your income tax return is not eligible for a SSN, you must obtain an Individual Taxpayer Identification Number (ITIN), a tax processing number for nonresident and resident aliens and their dependents. To obtain an ITIN, complete IRS *Form W-7, IRS Application for Individual Taxpayer Identification Number* (**www.irs.gov/pub/irs-pdf/iw7.pdf**) and submit it together with documentation substantiating foreign/alien status and identity for each individual.

If you have employees on your payroll or file pension or excise tax returns, you will need an Employer ID Number (EIN). You can obtain an EIN by filling out IRS Form SS-4 (**www.irs.gov/pub/irs-pdf/iss4.pdf**). All partnerships and corporations must have an EIN, and you must get a new EIN any time you change your business structure. If you are uncertain whether you need an EIN, consult *IRS Publication 1635: Understanding Your EIN* (**www.irs.gov/pub/irs-pdf/p1635.pdf**).

Beginning January 1, 2011, paid tax preparers must use a valid Preparer Tax Identification Number (PTIN) on returns they prepare. A PTIN can be obtained by registering on the IRS website (**www.irs.gov/taxpros/article/0,,id=210909,00.html**) and paying the $64.25 (2011) user fee. If you do not want to apply for a PTIN online, mail in *Form W-12, IRS Paid Preparer Tax Identification Number Application* (**www.irs.gov/pub/irs-pdf/fw12.pdf**). The paper application will take four to six weeks to process.

Do You Need an Accountant?

IRS tax forms come with detailed instructions that take you through each section, step by step. The IRS website offers dozens of publications, articles, and references that clarify common tax questions. Although you can order or download paper tax forms and fill them out manually, the IRS encourages you to file your taxes online (e-file). If you are comfortable with IRS paper forms, you can fill out the IRS Free File Fillable Forms online at **www.freefilefillableforms.com/FFA/Gateway/FED.htm**. Otherwise, you can use tax preparation software purchased at an office supply or electronics store, or online. Tax preparation software is designed to determine your eligibility for tax deductions by asking a series of questions. You enter information about your income and expenses, and it automatically calculates your deductions. Accountants use similar software to prepare their clients' tax returns. Before you start to file your business taxes yourself, ask yourself whether you will be able to comprehend the process without outside help. Many individuals are capable of filing their taxes properly but might not have the necessary insight to find all of the deductions that can save them money.

If your financial affairs are simple, you might be able to file your own taxes and claim deductions without difficulty. When you have income from multiple sources; expenses such as college tuition and health care; a complicated business; or unusual circumstances, such as a loss caused by a natural disaster or a recent divorce, a skilled accountant can help you file your taxes properly and find deductions. Filing your taxes correctly the first time will save you money and avoid problems with the IRS. An accountant can save you hours of research as you try to determine whether you qualify for certain deductions. The accountant can coach you as you organize your records and show you which deductions to claim. After one or two years, you might be able to do your own taxes by using your tax returns from previous years as a guide. Even if you use an accountant or part-time bookkeeper to manage your records and file taxes, learn as much as possible about the process. If you understand your taxes well, you will be more likely to find opportunities for legitimate tax deductions, and you will be more motivated to keep accurate records of your expenses. Knowledge of the tax code will also help you make future decisions about your business and your personal finances.

To find an accountant who knows about the tax issues affecting an online sales business, start by asking fellow business owners in your area or on online forums. Most online marketplaces have discussion groups and online communities of sellers who can make recommendations. Do an Internet search on websites such as CPAdirectory.com™ (**www.cpadirectory.com**) or the directory of the American Institute of CPAs (AICPA®) (**www.aicpa. org/ForThePublic/FindACPA/Pages/FindACPA.aspx**).

Basic accounting and tax preparation classes are offered at state or community colleges as well as local universities. SCORE (**www.score.org/events/ workshops**) and the U.S. Small Business Administration (SBA) (**www.sba. gov**) sponsor workshops, seminars, and classes about tax issues in many cities and online.

Filing Your Taxes

IRS Publication 334: Tax Guide for Small Business (**www.irs.gov/pub/irs-pdf/p334.pdf**) is a helpful resource. It gives a detailed explanation of the types of taxes you must file and advice about how to file them. Sometimes the language in IRS publications is difficult to decipher. If you have questions about the interpretation of a particular rule or requirement, you can often find simple explanations on the websites of accountants and business magazines by typing a phrase from the rule into an Internet search engine. Most tax preparation software allows you to e-mail questions to a tax expert or chat with one online. You also can consult an accountant or tax professional.

Filing electronically

The IRS encourages taxpayers to file their tax returns electronically using a computer. More than 105.5 million of the 132.4 million individual tax returns filed during the 2011 tax-filing season were filed electronically. Although you can still fill in the paper forms manually and mail them to the IRS, there are many advantages to filing electronically:

- **Accuracy** — In addition to the error checks built into return preparation software, additional checks are done during the transmission of software enabled e-file returns. Your chance of getting an error notice from the IRS is significantly reduced.

- **Security** — Your privacy and security are assured.

- **Paperless** — Eliminate paperwork by signing electronically with your own personal identification number (PIN) and filing a completely paperless return. Prepare your return using tax preparation software or a tax professional. There is nothing to mail.

- **Quick electronic confirmation** — You receive an electronic acknowledgment within 48 hours that the IRS has accepted your return for processing.

- **Fast refunds** — With IRS e-file, taxpayers get refunds in half the time it takes to file a paper tax return and receive a refund check. E-filers who choose direct deposit can receive their refund in as few as 10 days.

- **Free Internet filing options** — Use the IRS website, **www.irs.gov**, to access commercial tax preparation and e-file services available at no cost to eligible taxpayers.

- **Electronic payment** — Convenient, safe, and secure electronic payment options are available. E-file and options pay your taxes in a single step with a credit or debit card. By enrolling in the Electronic Federal Tax Payment System (EFTPS), taxpayers can make all federal tax payments online or by phone.

- **File now and pay later options** — Taxpayers can file early and pay later by scheduling an electronic funds withdrawal any time through April 15 of that year.

- **Convenient Federal/State e-filing** — Prepare and file your federal and state tax returns together. Taxpayers in 37 states and the District of Columbia can e-file their federal and state tax returns in one transmission to the IRS. The IRS forwards the state data to the appropriate state tax agency.

Most states also have electronic filing for income tax returns, and many local governments have forms that can be filled out and submitted online.

Information returns

The IRS requires you to report certain payments made or received by your business on forms called information returns. *Form 1099-MISC* is used for miscellaneous income including payments over $600 per year for services performed by subcontractors, accountants, attorneys, etc.; rent payments over $600; prizes or awards over $600; and royalty payments over $10. For example, if you hire an accounting student to help you set up your books and you pay him or her more than $600, you must report this to the IRS on a *Form 1099-MISC* and provide a copy to the student. If an acquaintance pays you more than $600 to take photos and set up a website and eBay listings for him, he must provide you with a copy of *Form 1099-MISC.*

You must obtain hard copies of IRS Form 1099-MISC

You can download and print a copy of IRS Form 1099-MISC from the IRS website (**www.irs.gov/pub/irs-pdf/f1099msc.pdf**) for your own information, but you cannot file it with the IRS because the IRS is not able to scan the printed version automatically. Instead, you must obtain a hard copy of the form. You can order official IRS forms online (**www.irs.gov/business-es/page/0,,id=23108,00.html**) or call (800) TAX-FORM (800-829-3676). IRS forms are often available free at post offices and public libraries. The IRS may impose a penalty of $50 per information return if you file forms that cannot be scanned.

Form W-2 must be used to report payments to employees (wages, tips, withheld income, Social Security, and Medicare). You can file Form W-2 online with the Social Security Administration (SSA) using its Business Services Online (**www.ssa.gov/bso/bsowelcome.htm**). The SSA reports some of the information on Form W-2 to the IRS. You will find instructions for filing W-2 forms in the IRS publication Instructions for Forms W-2 and W-3 (**www.irs.gov/instructions/iw2w3/index.html**).

Difference between an independent contractor and an employee

You might have questions about whether someone who is doing work for you is considered an employee or an independent contractor. Employees and independent contractors are treated differently according to labor laws, and their taxes are handled differently. An independent contractor is in business for himself or herself, makes quarterly income tax payments, and pays for his or her own Social Security and Medicare taxes, insurance, and benefits. Labor laws, such as wage and hour regulations, do not apply to a contractor, and he or she cannot claim unemployment insurance.

If you hire an employee, you must withhold personal income tax (both federal and state) from his or her paycheck. Half of the Social Security tax and the Medicare tax is deducted from the employee's wages, and you contribute the other half. As an employer, you contribute to the federal, and sometimes state, unemployment insurance system, and to state employment programs, such as disability or education and training. You also provide worker's compensation insurance for the employee in case an injury occurs during work. These benefits can add an additional 20 percent to 35 percent to the amount you spend on the employee's gross wages.

It is always a good idea to have an independent contractor sign a contract that clearly establishes the relationship between you and specifies the job responsibilities. When you hire a new employee, you must have him or her fill out a *Form I-9, Verification of Eligibility for Employment* and keep it on file. The employee must be able to submit a Social Security card, work permit, or other documentation proving he or she is eligible to work in the U.S. More detailed information is given online in the *U.S. Citizenship and Immigration Services Form 274, Handbook for Employers* (**www.uscis.gov/files/form/m-274.pdf**), or you can order a copy by phone at (800) 375-5283. New employees must also fill out an *IRS Form W-4*. If your employees qualify for and want to receive advanced earned income credit payments, they must give you a completed *Form W-5*.

Checklist for employee or independent contractor determination

For taxation purposes, the IRS uses the following questions to determine whether a worker is an employee or an independent contractor:

1. Do you have a written work agreement with the worker?
2. Is he or she a member of a union?
3. Do you set the worker's schedule?

4.   Does he provide similar services for others during the same time?

5.   Who buys materials?

6.   Who pays his or her helpers?

7.   Who provides the tools? The equipment?

8.   Do you reimburse him or her for expenses?

If you have a question about the status of a particular employee, you can request a determination from the IRS by filing a *Form SS-8, Determination of Worker Status for Purposes of Federal Employment Taxes and Income Tax Withholding* (**www.irs.gov/pub/irs-pdf/fss8.pdf**). For more information, refer to *IRS Pub 1779 Independent Contractor or Employee* (**www.irs.gov/pub/irs-pdf/p1779.pdf**).

Form 8300 is used to report cash payments over $10,000 from a buyer for a single transaction or two or more related transactions. The IRS defines cash as "the coins and currency of the United States and a foreign country," but it can also include cashier's checks, bank drafts, traveler's checks, and money orders with a face value of $10,000 or less. To determine whether you must file Form 8300, refer to the *IRS Workbook on Reporting Cash Payments of Over $10,000* (**www.irs.gov/businesses/small/article/0,,id=159755,00.html**).

When filling out your income tax return, you might have other personal transactions that should be reported on an information return, such as interest you paid on a student loan, debt cancellation or discharge, and IRA conversions or rollovers. You can find a complete list of these transactions and the correct forms to use in *A Guide to Information Returns* on the IRS website (**www.irs.gov/efile/article/0,,id=98114,00.html**). Most tax preparation software will alert you when you should use an information return to report a transaction.

Accounting Periods

When filing your taxes, you must decide on an accounting period, or tax year. An accounting period is the time interval over which you calculate your income and expenses. Once you have fixed on an accounting period, you must stick to it consistently. There are two different accounting periods: a calendar tax year or a fiscal tax year.

A calendar tax year is defined as "12 consecutive months beginning January 1 and ending December 31." You must choose the calendar tax year if you do not keep books, you do not have an annual accounting period, you have not been in business for 12 months at the time you do your taxes, or if you are required to use the calendar tax year under the Internal Revenue Code or the Income Tax Regulations. The IRS requires you to maintain your books and records, and report all of your income and expenses, for the period from January 1 through December 31.

A fiscal tax year is defined as "12 consecutive months ending on the last day of any month except December." A 52- to 53-week tax year is a fiscal tax year that begins and ends with a specific week every year and varies from 52 to 53 weeks. You are required to keep books and records and report all your business income and expenses for the fiscal tax year. A sole proprietor who uses a fiscal year rather than a calendar year must file an individual income tax return (including all the applicable schedules) no later than the 15th day of the fourth month after the end of the fiscal tax year.

For more information about accounting periods, refer to *IRS Publication 538: Accounting Periods and Methods* (**www.irs.gov/publications/p538/ar02.html#d0e147**).

If you begin doing business with one accounting period and then want to change your tax year, you will need to file IRS *Form 1128* (**www.irs.gov/pub/irs-pdf/f1128.pdf**).

Accounting Methods

The IRS defines accounting methods as "a set of rules used to determine when and how income and expenses are reported." These rules pertain to your overall accounting method as well as your treatment of individual items. You must choose an accounting method when you file your first income tax return on your Schedule C, and use that method when calculating your taxable income and keeping your books. You can, however, use different methods to account for your business and personal financial transactions.

The IRS accepts four accounting methods:

1.) Cash method

2.) Accrual method

3.) Special methods of accounting for certain items of income and expenses

4.) Combination method using elements of two or more of the above

Most sole proprietors use either the cash or accrual method. According to the IRS, most small business owners use the cash method, but it might not be appropriate for businesses that keep an inventory. Many online sales businesses require you to keep an inventory of some kind. You should choose an accounting system that fits the way you conduct your business. A cash system works well if you purchase a few items at a time and sell them quickly. However, if you spend tens of thousands of dollars in one year on materials and inventory that you are going to keep and sell for the next five years, your business will show a large loss the year you buy the inventory and excessive profits for the years after that when you are selling it off. This does not give you an accurate picture of your business finances or allow you to track exactly how much profit you make on each item in your inventory. An accrual system, on the other hand, breaks down the cost of materials, equipment, and inventory and distributes those costs over the years the inventory is being sold. Each year you report a portion of what you spent to acquire your inventory. Detailed information such as this can help you make important decisions about your business, such as whether to look for cheaper materials and negotiate for lower prices from your suppliers, raise or lower your prices, or buy less inventory.

A cash system may require extra bookkeeping to keep track of noncash items, such as receivables, payables, and depreciation of fixed assets, such as computers. You are allowed to use the cash method for your accounting and the accrual method to track sales and purchases of inventory.

In deciding which method to use, ask yourself:

- Do I expect my annual gross receipts to grow past $1 million?

  The IRS requires businesses with more than $1 million in annual gross receipts to use the accrual method. By starting out with the accrual accounting method, you will avoid having to make changes later.

- Will I be seeking bank loans, investors, or other sources of financing?

  If so, probably you will have to provide financial statements for audit or review by an independent accountant. Only an accrual system can create financial statements that comply with generally accepted accounting principles (GAAP).

The IRS allows you to use a combination of cash, accrual, and special methods of accounting as long the combination clearly shows your income and expenses, and you use it consistently. If you maintain an inventory, you generally must use an accrual method for purchases and sales, but you can use the cash method for all other items of income and expenses. If you use the cash method for figuring your income, you must use the cash method for reporting your expenses, and if you use an accrual method for reporting expenses, you must use an accrual method for calculating your income.

If you decide that you want to change your accounting method you first must request approval from the IRS by filling out and submitting *IRS Form 3115: Application for Change in Accounting Method* (**www.irs.gov/pub/irs-pdf/f3115.pdf**).

Cash method

The easiest of the four methods is the cash method. Your online business only reports sales when you receive cash from a buyer or a winning bidder. You do not record any checks or money orders until they arrive in your hands and you deposit them in the bank. It is almost like keeping a checking account.

To use the cash method correctly, you must consistently keep track of two accounts: income and expenses.

Income accounts include the gross income you received during your tax year, including any property or services. If you received property or services, then you will need to record the fair market value of those items in your records. (See *Barter* below.) Your income account must include constructive receipts — money that has been made available to you "without substantial limitations" even though you do not yet have physical possession of it. For example, a payment made to a third-party agent, such as PayPal or Amazon, is considered a constructive receipt because it belongs to you, even though you have not transferred it to your bank account or spent it yet. Another example would be a cashier's check sent to you by registered mail and waiting at the post office for you to pick it up. The money is available to you, even though you do not pick it up until several days later. This policy is intended to prevent taxpayers from lowering their taxable income by delaying receipt of money until after the end of the tax year. You are required to report income paid to you in the year that it was paid.

Expense accounts should record your expenses in the tax year in which you pay them. This includes expenses you intend to challenge in the next tax year, such as demanding a refund for faulty or damaged goods. (You will record that refund as income for the tax year in which you receive it.) When you pay expenses in advance, however, you can only deduct the portion that applies to the current tax year. For example, if you buy a one-year insurance policy that takes effect on July 1, you can deduct only half of the premium in the current tax year.

The cash method is relatively straightforward, but it is not appropriate for some businesses that keep an inventory or make product to sell. Corporations with average annual gross receipts exceeding $5 million, partnerships with corporations as partners that average annual gross receipts exceeding $5 million, and companies set up as tax shelters also cannot use the cash method.

If you receive more than $10 million in annual gross receipts, or if you spend more than $200,000 producing the goods you sell, you may be required to include indirect costs in the value of property you acquire or make for resale (See *Uniform capitalization* below).

Accrual method

The accrual method is used to "match income and expenses in the correct year." Under the accrual method, you must record any income that you made within a tax year. Sales are reported when they are completed, no matter the type of payment. If the winning bidder in an eBay auction pays with a check, you will report that sale as soon as the auction ends, not when you actually receive the check. Similarly, you record an expense when you incur it, even if you have not actually paid out the money yet. For example, if you buy materials to make a product on a credit account, you record the expense right away instead of waiting until you pay the monthly bill.

A transaction is recorded as income or an expense under the accrual method if it meets the "all-events test." The "all-events test" is met when all the events that establish a financial obligation have occurred, and the amount of the transaction can be determined with reasonable accuracy. For example, a buyer has placed an order, given shipping information and agreed to send a check within two business days. An expense is recorded as soon as "economic performance" occurs, meaning that services are performed or goods are received, even if you do not pay for them until later.

To use the accrual method, you must keep accurate records of your income, expenses, and inventories and be aware of uniform capitalization rules.

Income accounts using the accrual method record three dates for each receipt of income: the date you earn income by completing a sale, the date payment is due, and the date you actually receive the income. Although advance payments typically are reported in the tax year when you received them, in some cases, you can postpone reporting and paying taxes on them until the goods are delivered in the next tax year. One example is gift cards: a gift card is paid for in advance, but you can delay reporting it until you know exactly what items are purchased with it. For more details, refer to *IRS Publication 538: Accounting Periods and Methods* (**www.irs.gov/pub/irs-pdf/p538.pdf**).

Under the accrual method, you are allowed to deduct a business **expense** when all events have occurred that establish financial liability, the amount of that liability can be accurately determined, and economic performance has occurred. You cannot deduct an expense if you cannot prove that economic performance has occurred. For example, if you paid in advance for window-cleaning services, you cannot deduct that expense until the windows have been washed and you have a record such as a statement from the cleaning company. Expenses that are paid in advance only can be deducted in the year to which they apply. For example, if you pay in advance for five years of Internet hosting, you can only deduct one-fifth of the amount in each of the five years. The full amount of an advance payment for goods and services that meet the 12-Month Rule (they last for less than 12 months) can be recorded in the tax year the payment was made.

You cannot deduct business expenses that are owed to a related person (a sibling, spouse or former spouse, child or grandchild or adopted child and their spouses) who uses the cash method of accounting until you make a payment to that person.

The IRS requires you to evaluate your **inventory** and determine its value at the beginning and end of each tax year. Your inventory account includes all of your merchandise or stock in trade, any raw materials, any works you have in process, all finished products, and all supplies that will be a part of an item intended for sale. This includes packaging that will be part of your inventory, such as plastic bottles to contain hand lotions and the adhesive labels that will be stuck on the bottles. Your inventory records are necessary to calculate your income after production, a purchase, or a sale.

The IRS gives three methods for determining the value of your inventory: the cost method, lower of cost or market value method, and the retail method. The method you use depends on how your business is run and plays a role in determining your taxable income. The cost method values inventory based on the direct and indirect costs of acquiring or producing it. In the lower of cost or market value method, you compare the cost of acquiring each item in your inventory with its market value on the inventory date and choose the lower of the two amounts. In the retail method, you calculate your average markup percentage (the percentage you add to the wholesale price to get your retail selling price) for the year and subtract that markup from the retail value of your inventory at the end of the year to get the wholesale value of your inventory. *IRS Publication 538* gives step-by-step instructions for each method.

Cost method:

1. Take the value of your inventory at the end of the previous year.

2. Add:
   - The invoice price of any inventory items you purchased during the year, minus any discounts given to you by the supplier
   - The cost of shipping and storing the items

- All raw materials and supplies (not counting machinery and equipment that you will use for more than one year)
- All costs associated with manufacturing items for sale

3. Subtract:
   - Cost value of inventory sold during the year
   - Losses due to damaged or returned merchandise, or merchandise that had to be sold below cost because it was out of season, etc.

	Value of Beginning Inventory	$3,520
PLUS	Beads	$1,500
	Wire	$300
	Glue	$25
	Shipping	$75
	Electricity	$150
	Part-time labor	$600
	TOTAL	**$6,170**
MINUS	Cost of necklaces sold during year	$4,000
	Cost of necklaces damaged during shipment	$200
Value of Inventory at End of the Year		**$1,970**

Example: Cost method of valuing inventory

Lower of cost or market value method:

1. Determine the cost of acquiring or manufacturing each item in your inventory, and compare it to the item's current market value. The market value is the price you would pay to buy that item on the date you value your inventory.

2. Choose the lower of the cost or market value.

3. Each item in the inventory must be valued separately. You cannot add up the total cost value and the total market value of your inventory and then choose the lower of the two.

ITEM	COST	MARKET VALUE	INVENTORY VALUE
Cups	$100	$150	$100
Knives	$680	$600	$600
Pencils	$750	$900	$750
Bags	$1,200	$1,500	$1,200
Shirts	$2,800	$2,700	$2,700
Hats	$600	$400	$400
TOTAL	**$6,130**	**$6,250**	**$5,750**

Example: Choose the lower of cost or market value for each item in your inventory.

Retail method:

1. Calculate the total retail selling price of the items in your inventory at the beginning of the year. Add the total retail selling price of all the items you purchased during the year, adjusting for any markups or markdowns.

2. Subtract the cost of acquiring the items in your opening inventory plus the cost of the goods you acquired during the year.

3. To get your average markup percentage, divide the total in Step 2 by the total in Step 1.

4. Subtract your total retail sales for the year from the total in Step 1 to get the total retail value of your remaining inventory.

5. Multiply the retail value of your remaining inventory by the markup percentage from Step 3 to get the markup in your closing inventory.

6. Subtract the amount in Step 5 from the total retail value in Step 4 to get the approximate value of your closing inventory at cost.

	Retail value of beginning inventory	$3,750
PLUS	Retail value of inventory purchased during the year	$6,700
1. Total retail value of inventory		$10,450
MINUS	Cost value of beginning inventory	$2,450
MINUS	Cost value of inventory purchased during the year	$4,800
2. Total cost of inventory		$7,250
Total markup on inventory		$3,200
3. Markup percentage: $3,200/$10,450		30.62%
	Total retail value of inventory	$10,450
MINUS	Total retail sales for the year	$8,200
4. Retail value of remaining inventory		$2,250
MINUS	Markup on remaining inventory: 30.62% X $2,250	$689.00
5. Value of closing inventory at cost		$1,561.00

Uniform capitalization rules (UNICAP) require that you include in the cost of your inventory a portion of the indirect expenses your business incurs while producing or acquiring that inventory. These costs include administration expenses, quality control, rent, storage costs, pensions and benefits for employees, engineering and design, interest on loans, and franchising and license fees. However, the uniform capitalization rules do not apply if you use a simplified production method and your total indirect costs are $200,000 or less or if your average annual gross receipts are $10 million or less for the 3 previous tax years. These rules probably do not apply to you, at least not during the early years of your business. If you are bringing in $10 million a year in sales, you are likely to employ a full-time accountant to oversee your bookkeeping. The IRS gives step-by step instructions for capitalizing indirect costs in its publications *Capitalization Period of Direct and Indirect Costs* (**www.irs.gov/businesses/small/indus-**

tries/article/0,,id=97675,00.html) and *Cost Segregation Audit Technique Guide — Chapter 6.1 Uniform Capitalization* (**www.irs.gov/businesses/ article/0,,id=134361,00.html**).

Gains and Losses

According to the IRS, your business experiences a loss if the amount you spent operating your business (your adjusted basis) is more than the amount of income realized. You experience a gain if the amount realized is more than your adjusted basis.

The following definitions are taken from IRS Publication 334: Tax Guide for Small Business:

Basis — "The cost or purchase price of property is its basis for figuring the gain or loss from its sale or other disposition. However, if you acquired the property by gift, inheritance, or in some way other than buying it, you must use a basis other than its cost."

Adjusted Basis — "The adjusted basis of property is your original cost or other basis, plus certain additions such as administration costs and minus certain deductions such as depreciation and casualty losses. In determining gain or loss, the costs of transferring property to a new owner, such as selling expenses, are added to the adjusted basis of property."

Amount realized — "The amount you realize from a disposition is the total of all money you receive plus the fair market value of all property or services you receive."

Fair market value — "Fair market value is the price at which the property would change hands between a buyer and a seller, neither having to buy or sell, and both having reasonable knowledge of all necessary facts."

Amount recognized — "Your gain or loss realized from a disposition of property is a recognized gain or loss for tax purposes. Recognized gains must be included in gross income. Recognized losses are deductible from gross income. However, a gain or loss realized from certain exchanges of property is not recognized. Also, you cannot deduct a loss from the disposition of property held for personal use."

Gains and losses must be categorized as **ordinary** or **capital** so you can determine your net capital gain or loss. Ordinary and capital gains and losses are taxed at different rates and reported on different tax forms. Ordinary gain is income from wages, dividends, and interest on investments and is taxed at a higher rate. The sale of a capital asset results in a capital gain or loss. Just about everything you own and use for personal reasons or investments falls under the category of capital assets.

You also should determine if your gains and losses are **short term** or **long term**. If you buy and sell an item within one year, you have a short-term capital gain or loss. If you hold it for more than a year before selling it, you have a long-term capital gain or loss. For this reason, it is important to keep accurate records of your inventory so you know how long you held an item before selling it.

After you categorize your losses and gains, you should refer to Publication 334 (**www.irs.gov/pub/irs-pdf/p334.pdf**) and determine which forms you must use to file these items. Several different forms must be used depending on the type of loss or gain you are filing.

Barter Income

It is common for small business owners to exchange goods and services rather than paying for them. You might babysit a neighbor's child three mornings a week, and in exchange, she does some bookkeeping for you. Or you might trade some children's games for an antique doll. This type of exchange is called barter. You might think that such transactions are "off the books" because no money changes hands, but the IRS expects you to include the fair market value (FMV) of goods and services received in exchange for goods or services you provide in your income for that year. This income is reported on *Form 1040, Schedule C Profit or Loss from Business* (**www.irs.gov/pub/irs-pdf/f1040sc.pdf**).

Internet barter exchanges allow members to buy and sell goods and services among themselves using assigned dollar values called "trade units." Barter exchanges such Barter Systems Inc. (**www.bartersys.com/index.asp**) and BarterQuest® (**www.barterquest.com**) act as bookkeepers, keeping track of trade dollars that participants accumulate. Earning trade or barter dollars through a barter exchange is considered taxable income, just as if your product or service was sold for cash. Barter exchanges are required to issue *Form 1099-B Proceeds from Broker and Barter Exchange Transactions* (**www.irs.gov/pub/irs-pdf/f1099b.pdf**), annually to their clients or members and to the IRS. You must include barter income from an Internet barter exchange in your taxable income.

If you barter depreciated business assets, such as an old computer or fax machine, you might have capital gains, ordinary gains, and depreciation recapture to report. If you have barter transactions of appreciated assets, such as art, antiques, and collectibles where the fair market value is more than your cost or other basis, you usually will have a reportable gain. These gains may be business income or capital gains, depending on whether they were part of your business inventory or personal possessions. For more information, see the IRS article, *Bartering Income* (**www.irs.gov/businesses/small/article/0,,id=187904,00.html**).

CHAPTER 4

Business Deductions — A Lifeline for Sole Proprietors

The advantage of conducting your Internet sales as a business rather than a hobby is that you are entitled to deduct business expenses from your taxable income. The IRS defines a business deduction as "all the ordinary and necessary expenses paid or incurred during the taxable year in carrying on any trade or business." To claim an item as a deduction, you must determine if the item is an ordinary or necessary expense. The IRS defines an ordinary expense as "one that is common and accepted in a trade or business." A necessary expense is "one that is helpful and appropriate for a trade or business."

IRS publications, articles, and other documents provide valuable information about tax laws and your rights. Make sure you are looking at the most up-to-date versions available. Protocols, income limits, amounts, and eligibility for deductions change almost every year. Avoid mishaps and errors by following the current version of the rules.

This chapter explains how business deductions can save you a lot of money. You must learn to differentiate between different types of income that are taxed at different rates and learn what is deductible as a business expense and what is not. By understanding business deductions in advance, you can plan and look for potential tax savings. All business expenses and deductions must be backed up with solid evidence, such as records, receipts, and bank statements.

Types of Income

Several types of income are reported on your tax returns. Each type is taxed differently; some income is taxed at a much higher rate. Learning to differentiate among types of income will help you determine what to do with the money your business earns so you can keep as much of it as possible. If you have a profitable year, you can reduce your tax liability by moving some of the money you earn into investments taxed at lower rates. If your personal finances are complex, a tax accountant or a financial planner can help you set up investment accounts and find investments that will allow you to keep more of your money and save for the future.

Earned income

Earned income refers to any money your business earns by performing services or selling goods to clients. Earned income includes any income you earn by working for someone else, such as salaries, wages, tips, and professional fees; and farm income. Income from partnerships, S corporations, trusts, and estates is earned income only if you actively participate in the business that provides the income.

Earned income generally is taxed at a higher rate than other types of income and is eligible for fewer deductions.

Alternative Minimum Tax (AMT)

In 1969, Congress created the alternative minimum tax (AMT) after Treasury Secretary Joseph Barr announced that 155 high-income households in the U.S. had paid no federal income taxes at all, because they were able to claim so many tax deductions and exemptions. Its purpose is to ensure high-income households pay at least some income tax. Essentially, the AMT is a parallel system for calculating income tax. It strips away the deductions, exclusions, exemptions, and credits that reduce taxable income under the regular income tax system, subtracts its own standard deduction, and calculates tax as a percentage (26 percent of income up to $175,000 plus 28 percent of income over $175,000) of the remaining income. You are required to pay whichever amount is higher: regular income tax or the AMT.

Though originally designed to target only the wealthiest households, the AMT was not indexed (adjusted) for inflation. Therefore, as the average annual income of U.S. households has increased over the years, more and more upper-middle-class taxpayers have had to pay it. Every year, Congress has to enact legislation to prevent the AMT from reverting to its original levels and affecting large numbers of taxpayers. In 1970, about 20,000 taxpayers paid the AMT. In 2009, this number had grown to about 4 million.

In 2011, if you are single and your income is greater than $48,450, married filing jointly with an income greater than $74,450, or married filing separately with an income greater than $37,225, you may have to pay the AMT. The AMT particularly affects couples with several children, taxpayers who live in states with high income tax, and taxpayers who would benefit under the regular tax system from large amounts of itemized deductions, net operating losses (NOLs), deductions for mortgage interest on home equity loans, long-term capital gains and other substantial deductions or credits. All of these circumstances would substantially lower their taxable income under the regular income tax system, but the AMT either eliminates these credits and deductions or makes them much smaller. As a result, they must pay the higher AMT instead of regular income tax.

The AMT is calculated using *IRS Form 6251: Alternative Minimum Tax— Individuals* (**www.irs.gov/pub/irs-pdf/f6251.pdf**). Most tax preparation software automatically determines whether you must pay the AMT and calculates it for you. If you are filling out a tax return manually, the IRS has an online worksheet. *Alternative Minimum Tax (AMT) Assistant for Individuals* (**www.irs.gov/businesses/small/article/0,,id=150703,00.html**), to quickly determine if you must pay the AMT. *Instructions for Form 1040* (**www.irs.gov/pub/irs-pdf/i1040.pdf**) also contains an AMT worksheet.

If there is a possibility that you might have to pay the AMT, you can do a few things to reduce your deductions and exemptions under the regular income tax rules or reduce your taxable income under the AMT:

Keep your state and local tax deduction as small as possible. Do not prepay property taxes, and if you are withholding state income tax, do not overpay. Pay only what you owe.

Sell your exercised incentive stock options (ISOs) in the same year you exercise them. An ISO, given only to employees of a company, is the option to buy shares of that company's stock at a set price rather than the market price. If you have been given an ISO by your employer and you decide to exercise the option and buy stock at the set price, then the AMT treats the difference between the fixed exercise price and the market price as taxable income, while regular income tax does not. If you sell the stock in the same year you bought it, however, the profit is taxable under the regular income tax system but not under the AMT.

Portfolio income

Portfolio income is the money you make through various investments, capital gains, interest, royalties, and stock dividends. Capital gain is the profit you make from selling items, property or stocks that you have held for more than one year. Interest is the income you receive from bonds, bank Certificates of Deposits (CDs), money market and savings accounts, and loans to others. Dividends are the payments a company makes to its shareholders. Different types of portfolio income are taxed at different rates. Dividends and capital gains are taxed at a lower rate than interest income. Profit from short-term capital gains (assets that you bought and sold within 12 months) is taxed at your regular income tax rate, while the tax rate for profit from long-term capital gains (assets that you held for more than 12 months before selling them) is between 10 percent and 23.8 percent, depending on your income tax bracket. Capital gains from the sale of collectibles are taxed at a higher rate of 28 percent. *Chapter 7 discusses more about capital gains tax on collectibles.*

Portfolio income is not subject to Social Security or Medicare taxes. Also, capital gains in a portfolio can be offset by capital losses — the amount you lose when you sell an asset for less than what you paid for it.

To increase your portfolio income, invest some of your earned income in a stock portfolio. Contributions to a 401(k) plan, a Roth IRA, a Roth 401(k), or a Traditional IRA confer certain tax advantages. *Chapter 12 discusses how you can reduce your taxable income by investing in a tax-advantaged portfolio.*

Passive income

Passive income comes from business investments in which you do not actively participate, such as purchasing an office building and renting out offices or becoming a financial partner in a partnership operated by the other partners. You only are allowed to deduct passive income losses equal to or less than the amount of passive income you received that tax year. You can carry these losses forward, however, until you either sell the investment or make enough money to deduct the losses in a future tax year. If you are actively involved in renting out a real estate investment, and your AGI is less than $150,000, you can reduce your passive income by up to $25,000 to cover costs and expenses.

Tax laws probably will change

Many provisions of the tax laws expired or were phased out in 2010, and Congress is constantly enacting new legislation to either increase federal tax revenue or stimulate the economy by providing tax relief to businesses and individuals. Income limits, eligibility, and the amounts of some tax credits are currently under debate. Some of the current rules might change by the time you file your next tax return. Keep abreast of the newest developments by reading tax blogs and IRS articles.

Income Tax Brackets

Your federal income tax bracket is the highest percentage tax rate that you are taxed on any of your annual adjusted income. If you are in the 35 percent tax bracket, it does not mean you pay 35 percent of your entire income in taxes. In 2007, if you were married filing jointly, then you would have been taxed 10 percent on the first $15,650, 15 percent on the next $48,050 ($63,700 minus $15,650), and so on. You would have paid 35 percent only on the amount over $349,700.

Federal Income Tax Brackets for 2008 - 2010

Tax Rate	MARRIED FILING JOINTLY			SINGLE FILERS		
	2008 Taxable Income	2009 Taxable Income	2010 Taxable Income	2008 Taxable Income	2009 Taxable Income	2010 Taxable Income
10%	Not over $16,050	Not over $16,700	Not over $16,750	Not over $8,025	Not over $8,350	Not over $8,375
15%	$16,050 - $67,100	$16,700 - $67,900	$16,750 - $68,000	$8,025 - $32,550	$8,350 - $33,950	$8,375 - $34,000
25%	$67,100 - $131,450	$67,900 - $137,050	$68,000 - $137,300	$32,550 - $78,850	$33,950 - $82,250	$34,000 - $82,400
28%	$131,450 - $200,300	$137,050 - $208,850	$137,300 - $209,250	$78,850 - $164,550	$82,250 - $171,550	$82,400 - $171,850

Tax Rate	MARRIED FILING JOINTLY			SINGLE FILERS		
	2008 Taxable Income	2009 Taxable Income	2010 Taxable Income	2008 Taxable Income	2009 Taxable Income	2010 Taxable Income
33%	$200,300 - $375,000	$208,850 - $372,950	$209,250 - $373,650	$164,500 - $357,700	$171,550 - $372,950	$171,850 - $373,650
35%	Over $372,500	Over $372,950	Over $373,650	Over $357,700	Over $372,950	Over $373,650

Federal income tax brackets are adjusted every year for inflation. You can find an updated federal tax bracket calculator on efile.com (**www.efile.com/tax-service/tax-calculator/tax-brackets**). By looking at the chart above, you can see that any amount of income that raises you into a higher tax bracket will be taxed at the higher rate. For example, in 2010 if you had income from other sources such as wages, Social Security, or interest on savings bonds of $8,000, and you had income of $12,500 from your Internet sales business, you would end up paying taxes of 15 percent on $12,125 of that $20,500 income. When your income level is hovering near the top of the second income tax bracket, you might be able to save yourself an extra 10 percent in taxes on income that exceeds $34,000 if you can find a few extra deductions. And perhaps you can delay cashing in savings bonds until early in the next tax year or work fewer hours in a part-time job to lower your overall income.

Your tax bracket is based on your taxable income, which is your actual income reduced by a number of deductions. These include a personal exemption for each person filing and each dependent ($3,700 in 2010), a standard deduction ($11,600 for married couples filing jointly in 2010), or itemized deductions for mortgage interest, medical expenses, and local and state income taxes. Self-employed individuals and couples may be able to deduct business expenses. There is an Earned Income Tax Credit (EITC) ($5,036 in 2010 for families with two children) for moderate and low-income working parents with children, and deductions for child-care or dependent-care expenses. And of course, if you still have earned income, you can subtract contributions to a traditional IRA. Retired individuals who no longer have earned income or dependent children living with them are not able to take many tax deductions, but their younger beneficiaries who are still raising families will probably be in the lower tax brackets.

Tax Deductions and Exemptions

A tax deduction is an expense subtracted from a taxpayer's gross income to lower taxable income. Numerous tax deductions are available to individuals and businesses, but the IRS rules defining them are strict and detailed. Knowing in advance about the various deductions and how to qualify for them will save you tax dollars and keep you out of trouble if the IRS selects you for an audit. Tax preparation software is designed to identify possible deductions and walk you through the calculations on tax forms, but you must have accurate documentation to back them up. Chapter 2 explained the importance of keeping records of your expenses and filing receipts, invoices, and other documents where you can access them easily.

Detailed information about tax deductions and exemptions can be found in *IRS Pub 501: Exemptions, Standard Deduction and Filing Information* (**www.irs.gov/pub/irs-pdf/p501.pdf**). You are required to report and pay income tax on your AGI (adjusted gross income). For a self-employed online seller, this means the gross income from your business, plus any income from wages or salaries, investments, and "incidental or outside operations or sources" and minus all deductions and exemptions.

Section 26 U.S.C. § 151 of the *Internal Revenue Code (IRC)* provides for a personal tax exemption for each person in the taxpayer's household. The U.S. government believes that a certain amount of each person's income should be exempt from taxes. The tax exemption is roughly equivalent to the minimum amount of money a person would need to subsist for a year. In 2010, the exemption for each person was $3,650. *IRS Pub 501* gives detailed instructions for determining who qualifies for a personal exemption on your tax return.

Standard and itemized deductions

Tax deductions are amounts you are allowed to subtract from your taxable income to compensate for certain expenses. A business is allowed to deduct expenses incurred to produce income. An individual may be allowed to deduct expenses related to activities that the government wants to encourage or support, such as the purchase of health insurance, recovery from a natural disaster, college tuition, state income tax, and charitable giving.

The IRS provides two ways to calculate deductions: You either can take a standard deduction or itemize your expenses by listing each one individually. You only will benefit from taking the standard deduction if it exceeds the total amount of your allowable itemized deductions. The amount of the standard deduction is adjusted each year for inflation. The amount of your standard deduction will depend on your filing status and your age. Standard deductions are higher for someone who is older than 65, blind, suffered a net loss due to a federally declared disaster, or paid excise taxes on the purchase of new vehicle. You are not eligible for the standard deduction if:

1. You are married, filing a separate return, and your spouse itemizes deductions

2. You are filing a tax return for a short tax year because of a change in your annual accounting period

3. You are a nonresident or dual-status alien during the calendar year

The IRS identifies seven circumstances in which you will benefit by taking itemized deductions:

1. You do not qualify for the standard deduction, or the amount you can claim is limited

2. You paid more than 7.5 percent of your adjusted gross income in medical and dental expenses during the year

3. You paid mortgage interest on up to $1 million in home loan debt and/or up to $100,000 in home equity loan debt, and/or paid taxes on your home

4. You had large unreimbursed employee business expenses or other miscellaneous deductions

5. You had large uninsured casualty or theft losses

6. You made large contributions to qualified charities

7. You have total itemized deductions that are more than the standard deduction

Because of the nature of an online sales business, there is a good possibility that you will be able to deduct more if you itemize deductions. Tax preparation software walks you through each possible deduction, and based on the information you enter, it calculates whether you should take the standard deduction or itemized deductions. You also can report your itemized deductions manually on *Schedule A* and attach it to *Form 1040*. If you qualify for the higher standard deduction for new motor vehicle taxes or a net disaster loss, you must attach *Schedule L*. Tax Forms and instructions are available on the IRS website (**www.irs.gov**). You can order them by phone or pick them up from post offices and public libraries.

PEP and Pease could limit the amount of your exemptions and deductions

Personal exemptions are intended to relieve some of the tax burden on low-income taxpayers, and deductions are designed to promote certain types of spending. About 20 years ago, to increase federal tax revenue, Congress enacted PEP (personal exemption phase-out) and Pease (limitation on Itemized deductions, named after its author, Representative Donald Pease) to phase out the exemptions available to high-income taxpayers. Beginning in 2006,

PEP and Pease gradually were repealed, until in 2010 there were no income restrictions at all. The Obama Budget calls for these restrictions to be reinstated, so if you are a single taxpayer with an AGI more than $200,000 or a couple with an AGI more than $250,000, you may not be able to claim these deductions starting in 2011. Pease reduces most itemized deductions by 3 percent of the amount by which AGI exceeds the threshold, up to a maximum reduction of 80 percent of itemized deductions.

Not all deductions are restricted; the restrictions do not apply to deductions for medical expenses, investment interest, casualty and theft losses, and gambling losses (which can only offset gambling winnings included in income). It does apply to deductions for mortgage interest, charitable gifts, and state and local taxes, as well as more obscure deductions for union dues, tax preparation fees, and safety deposit box expenses. The greatest criticism of Pease is that it makes the tax code more complex and amounts to an increase in the tax rate for high-income taxpayers.

Business Expenses

A business expense is not deducted directly from your taxable income, but from your business income. The IRS allows you to deduct the cost of carrying on a trade or business from the income produced by that business, as long as the business is operated to make a profit. You can reduce your taxable income by subtracting business expenses from your business income to diminish your net profit from the business. Many costs can be deducted as business expenses if you are aware of them and document them properly.

Business expenses are reported on *Schedule C* and attached to your *Form 1040*. Tax preparation software will help you identify and calculate your business expenses.

As Chapter 2 explains, you must keep receipts and documentation to verify each of your business expenses. It is common for taxpayers to try to reduce their taxable income by fabricating or inflating business expenses. The IRS watches for red flags — abnormal expense amounts that suggest a taxpayer is being dishonest. Reporting fabricated expenses makes your tax return suspect when it is compared to the returns of other taxpayers in similar businesses. If the IRS audits you and finds you have falsified your expense records, you will have to pay penalties in addition to the income tax you owe on the disallowed expenses.

What You Cannot Deduct

One of the most frequent tax errors made by self-employed individuals is taking a deduction from business income for personal compensation and time spent working in the business. Although you spend much of your time tending to your business, you cannot deduct that time as a business expense because you are self-employed. The exception to this rule is if your business is structured as a corporation. Then you can hire yourself as an employee and deduct your salary under the employee deduction.

Other expenses you might think you can deduct as business expenses, such as estimated tax payments, life insurance premiums, meals, campaign contributions, grooming expenses, and commuting expenses, are considered personal expenses by the IRS and cannot be deducted from your business income.

Capital expenses are purchases of fixed assets used to operate your business, such as computers, desks, fax machines, or sewing machines used to

make the product you sell. A good rule of thumb is that an asset is a capital expense if it has a useful life of more than one year. For example, office supplies are not a capital expense because you ordinarily use them up within a short time. Capital expenditures typically are depreciated over the life of the asset. For example, you subtract a portion of the value of a computer each of the five years that it remains in service. Instructions for tax forms include formulas for calculating depreciation, and tax preparation software calculates it automatically.

The expenses used to figure the cost of goods sold by your business should be recorded as inventory and are not part of your business expenses. Many people illegally deduct items they should not because they confuse business expenses with inventory. Products you buy for resale; raw materials; the cost of shipping and storing these items; and indirect costs, such as the rental of factory space, factory utilities, and direct labor costs (including contributions to pensions or annuity plans) for workers who produce the products are part of your cost of goods sold, not business expenses.

Many online sellers charge their customers shipping and handling fees in excess of the actual shipping cost to increase their profit on a sale. In some cases, you might sell an item for less than a dollar and make all your profit from the shipping charges. You cannot deduct the amount you charged your customers for shipping and handling as a business expense, only the amount that you actually paid for packaging materials, postage, and shipping.

Inflated shipping and handling fees can hurt your business

Although inflating shipping and handling fees is not illegal, you might experience negative results on your online marketplaces. Customers could post negative feedback when you overcharge for shipping and handling fees and give your business a bad image. The increased shipping fee could raise your price above a competitor's price for the same item and prompt a customer to cancel the sale. In extreme cases, you even could be kicked off your online marketplace. It is better to be honest and not charge excessively for shipping and handling.

What You Can Deduct

The IRS allows many kinds of business expenses. The expenses you can claim depend on the nature of your product and the way you conduct your business. You might be able to recharacterize a personal expense as a business expense by making some simple changes, such as setting aside a dedicated room in your home for your business.

IRS Publication 535: Business Expenses (**www.irs.gov/businesses/small/ article/0,,id=109807,00.html**) explains in detail how to determine which expenses are deductible as business expenses.

The most common categories of business deductions for small businesses are:

- Automobiles
- Advertising
- Donations and gifts
- State and local taxes
- Bad debt
- Thefts and losses
- Consignment
- Education
- Inventory
- Employees
- Travel
- Entertainment
- Fees and licenses

Automobiles

If your vehicle is used for business purposes, and you can prove it, you can make several deductions from your business income. There are two ways to calculate business expenses related to the use of your vehicle: mileage allowances and vehicle expenses. The mileage allowance allows you to deduct a specified amount for each mile you drive for business purposes. The amount per mile changes every year, so refer to *Standard Mileage Rates* (**www.irs.gov/taxpros/article/0,,id=156624,00.html**) for the latest information.

If you drive your vehicle for both business and personal use, you will not be able to deduct 100 percent of your vehicle expenses. Keep track of how often you use your vehicle for business purposes to maximize the amount you can deduct. A good way to do this is to keep a mileage log, a notebook in which you recording the mileage on your car's odometer at the beginning and end of each trip. Special mileage logs that fit conveniently in your glove box are sold on eBay and at office supply stores for $2 to $7.

The IRS gives specific examples of using your vehicle for business as opposed to personal use. Examples of business use are driving to and from the post office to mail packages to customers or pick up business-related packages; driving to a customer's home or meeting them to allocate a package; and driving to a business meeting with a particular organization. If you operate your online sales business outside of your home in a separate office space, you will not be allowed to deduct any miles driven on trips originating from your office. This means that only the miles you drive from your home to do business-related activities would be deductible.

To use the "actual cost method," keep track of the miles you drive your vehicle for business purposes and for personal use, and calculate the percentage of business use. Keep detailed records and receipts for gas, oil changes, tires, insurance fees, repairs, license fees, and depreciation costs associated with the vehicle. You can deduct a portion of those expenses equal to the percentage of business use. For example, if you drive your vehicle for business 80 percent of the time, and for personal use 20 percent of the time, you can deduct 80 percent of the costs associated with operating your vehicle.

If you lease a vehicle, you can deduct a percentage of each lease payment as a business expense. When a vehicle is leased for more than 30 days, you may have to add an "inclusion amount" to your income for each year that you hold the lease. You can find more information about leasing a vehicle in *IRS Publication 463: Travel, Entertainment, Gift, and Car Expenses* (**www.irs.gov/publications/p463/index.html**).

Advertising

The IRS knows you will need to advertise your products for your Internet sales business to prosper. Advertising counts as a business expense. The IRS allows you to deduct advertising costs for business cards, fliers, brochures, signs, billboards, ads in phone books, ads on the radio or TV, and Internet advertising. You can deduct consulting fees for your business' website, website design, market research expenses, and design costs for advertisements, a logo or letterhead as part of your marketing expenses.

Donations and gifts

You or your Internet sales business can deduct charitable donations of cash or property ("in-kind" contributions) to a qualified charitable organization. Donations to needy individuals are not tax deductible. You also can deduct mileage and other travel expenses incurred while volunteering for a charitable organization, based on the IRS-designated standard mileage rate for charitable work. You cannot deduct money for your time spent working for the organization, such as time spent serving on a board. If you receive something in return for your donation, such as candy or tickets to a gala event, you must subtract its value from the amount you deduct. In-kind donations may be deducted at the fair market value of the property at the time of the contribution. If the value of your noncash donation exceeds $500, it must be reported on *IRS Form 8283: Noncash Charitable Contributions* (**www.irs.gov/pub/irs-pdf/f8283.pdf**) and attached to your *Form 1040*.

You must document your contributions with receipts, canceled checks, letters of acknowledgment, and other written confirmation. The deduction must be taken in the year the donation was actually paid, not the year it was pledged. The way you take the deduction for charitable donations depends on how your business is structured. If you are running your on-line sales business as a corporation, your business is allowed to deduct its charitable donations from its business income. You cannot deduct dona-tions from your business income if your business is a sole proprietorship, partnership, or LLC. Instead, you take a personal income tax deduction for charitable donations. Charitable donations must be itemized, and the total amount of your itemized deductions must equal more than 2 percent of your personal AGI. If you are a partnership, you can divide the amount to be deducted among the partners, who can each report a portion of the donation on their tax returns.

The IRS guidelines for deducting business gifts are found in *IRS Publication 463*. You cannot deduct more than $25 in one tax year for business gifts you give, directly or indirectly, to each individual. An indirect gift is "one intended for the eventual personal use or benefit of a particular person." When you give a gift to a company that is intended for a particular person or group of people, such as the company's managers or sales staff, it is considered an indirect gift. A gift given to a customer's family member is considered an indirect gift to that customer, unless you have a separate business relationship with the family member. The $25 limit does not ap-ply to incidental costs, such as engraving or wrapping paper, that do not add value to the gift.

If you and your spouse both give gifts to someone, you are treated as one taxpayer and can take only one $25 deduction. The same is true for part-ners in a partnership.

If you give a restaurant gift card or a theater ticket to a customer, you can treat it either as a gift or as an entertainment expense. If you accompany the customer to the restaurant or theater, however, it must be treated as an entertainment expense.

State and local taxes

You are allowed to deduct various state and local taxes from your taxable income. You can deduct sales tax you paid on items bought for resale online, use taxes you paid on items you bought out-of-state, personal property taxes for any equipment or supplies, inventory taxes at the end of the year, and up to half of your self-employment tax. These deductions are calculated on your state and local income tax forms.

Bad debt

The IRS knows that your business occasionally will suffer losses and allows you to deduct these amounts from taxable income. When someone owes you money and you cannot collect it, you have bad debt. In an Internet sales business, bad debt can occur if a buyer's check bounces, customers reverse credit card transactions with chargebacks and keep the merchandise, you send goods to customers who never pay you, or a customer pays with a stolen credit card. To deduct the bad debt, you previously must have included the amount in your income. You have to show that the debt is worthless — that you took all reasonable steps to collect the debt and there is no chance of it being repaid. You do not have to sue the customer in court. A business debt can be partially worthless if the customer pays only part of what he or she owes. In that case, you can deduct only the worthless portion of the debt. Business bad debts are reported as ordinary losses on *Form 1040* using *Schedule C*. An ordinary loss is any loss that is not a result of the sale or exchange of a capital asset.

Debt that is not related to your business, such as a loan to a friend, is considered nonbusiness debt. You can deduct nonbusiness debt from your personal taxable income if you can prove that you expected the debt to be paid back and the surrounding facts and circumstances indicate there is no reasonable expectation of payment. For example, your brother might have signed a written agreement to repay the $5,000 you loaned him two months before he declared bankruptcy and suffered a disabling stroke. The written agreement is proof that you expected repayment, and the bankruptcy and your brother's medical condition clearly demonstrate that he is unable to do so. You cannot deduct a partially worthless nonbusiness debt. A nonbusiness bad debt is reported as a short–term capital loss in Part 1 on *Form 1040, Schedule D: Capital Gains and Losses*. (**www.irs.gov/pub/irs-pdf/f1040sd.pdf**). It is subject to the capital loss limitations. A nonbusiness bad debt deduction requires a separate detailed statement attached to your return.

Thefts and losses

Losses due to theft or casualty can be deducted from either business income or personal income, depending on whether the loss is a business or a personal loss. The IRS defines casualty as "the damage, destruction, or loss of property resulting from an identifiable event that is sudden, unexpected, or unusual," such as a car accident, earthquake, fire, storm, hurricane, or flood. Damage caused by gradual deterioration, such as a termite infestation, is not deductible. Neither is damage caused by a new and untrained puppy because that kind of damage is not unexpected or unusual. Arson and accidents caused by a willful or deliberate act do not qualify.

A theft is the "illegal taking and removing of money or property with the intent to deprive the owner of it." For damage or theft of personal property, calculate the loss by subtracting any compensation you received from insurance from whichever is lower: your adjusted basis in the property before the loss or the difference between the fair market value (FMV) of the property before the theft or casualty and its FMV after the loss. Your adjusted basis is the amount you spent to acquire it, plus the cost of any improvements and additions. The FMV of a stolen item after a theft is considered zero because you no longer have the item to sell. That means your loss deduction equals the amount you spent to acquire and improve the item, minus any compensation you might receive from insurance. The antique vase you bought ten years ago for $15 (your adjusted basis) might now be worth $200 on the market, but if it is stolen, you only can deduct $15 for your loss.

There are restrictions on deducting losses of personal property. The $100 rule allows you to deduct only losses in excess of $100. If the value of the lost or damaged items was less than $100, then you cannot deduct anything, and you must subtract $100 from the items' value when you report the loss. The $100 rule applies to all the damage caused by a single casualty — you subtract the $100 from the total value of all the items lost, not from the value of each item. Two related casualties, such as a storm and flood or a house fire and smoke damage, are regarded as a single event, so you deduct the $100 only once. Currently, Congress is debating whether to raise the amount from $100 to $500. Check the IRS website (**www.irs.gov**) for up-to-date information.

The 10-percent rule requires you to subtract 10 percent of your AGI from the reported loss — in other words, you only get a tax deduction for the amount exceeding 10 percent of your AGI, plus $100. Suppose a tornado destroys your garage and causes $5,000 in damage. Your AGI for the year is $25,000. You can deduct $2,400, the amount left after you subtract $100 and 10 percent of your AGI ($2,500) from $5,000.

Total Damage	**$5,000**
Minus $100	$100
	$4,900
Minus 10% of $25,000 AGI	$2,500
Total Deduction	**$2,400**

If you suffer loss or damage to a property that was partly for business use and partly for personal use, such as a home in which you have a home office, the personal and business losses must be figured separately. The $100 rule and the 10-percent rule do not apply to business losses.

A loss of business property is calculated by taking your adjusted basis in the property and subtracting the value of anything that can be salvaged and any compensation you received from insurance. If more than one item has been damaged or stolen, you must calculate your loss for each item individually. There is an exception for personal-use real property, such as your home. In that case, the value of buildings, storage sheds, trees, and landscaping all can be recorded as a single loss.

Proof of loss

From *IRS Publication 547: Casualties, Disasters and Thefts*

To deduct a casualty or theft loss, you must be able to show that there was a casualty or theft. You also must be able to support the amount you take as a deduction.

Casualty loss proof. For a casualty loss, you should be able to show all the following:

- The type of casualty (car accident, fire, storm, etc.) and when it occurred

- That the loss was a direct result of the casualty

- That you were the owner of the property, or if you leased the property from someone else, that you were contractually liable to the owner for the damage

- Whether a claim for reimbursement exists for which there is a reasonable expectation of recovery

Theft loss proof. For a theft loss, you should be able to show all the following:

- When you discovered that your property was missing

- That your property was stolen

- That you were the owner of the property

- Whether a claim for reimbursement exists for which there is a reasonable expectation of recovery

The cost of photos and appraisals done to show the condition and value of your property before/after it was damaged or stolen is an expense and cannot be included in your loss. Instead, these expenses must be recorded as business expenses or as itemized deductions on your tax return.

Money for incidental expenses, such as a rental car or medical care after an accident or repairs to a lock after a theft, cannot be deducted as part of your loss. If the loss or damage was to a business property, you can deduct them as business expenses.

Recording inventory losses

Theft or damage to items in your inventory can be reported in one of two ways:

Increase the cost of goods sold in your inventory account by correctly reporting your opening and closing inventory. Any compensation or reimbursement you receive for the loss must be subtracted from the cost of goods sold. Do not claim an additional loss for theft or damage.

Delete the damaged or stolen inventory from your opening inventory, and deduct the loss separately. Any compensation or reimbursement must be subtracted from the amount of the loss. Do not report the compensation as income. If you have not received an insurance payment by the end of the tax year but you know you are going to receive it, subtract that amount from the loss.

Losses and gains are reported on *IRS Form 4684: Casualties and Thefts* (**www.irs.gov/pub/irs-pdf/f4684.pdf**). A loss also is reported as an itemized deduction on *Schedule A*. If you experience a gain because your insurance pays you more than your adjusted basis in the lost property, you must report that on *Schedule D*.

Online selling fees

For each transaction in an online marketplace, you must pay subscriptions, listing fees, and commissions. Many sales platforms charge extra for extra graphics, pictures, logos, and enhanced or featured listings. Costs that can be deducted as business expenses include PayPal fees, insertion fees, enhancement options on listings, final value fees, and merchant account transactions.

Increase income with cash-back bonuses

You can increase your income if you use a PayPal ATM card, which entitles you to a cash-back bonus of between 1 percent and 1.5 percent. Add up your cash-back bonuses, and report them as "other income" on your *Schedule C.*

Consignment

Consigned goods are goods that you own and you give to someone called a consignor to sell on your behalf. The consignor typically takes a commission from the sale price. According to IRS document *FS-2007-23* "all income from auctions, traditional or online, and consignment sales generally is taxable unless certain exceptions are met."

Because your consignment sales are part of your business, you can report all the costs related to consignment sales as business expenses, including storage fees for consignment inventory. Your total consignment sales should be reported as income, and the cost of acquiring the goods you consign should be recorded in your inventory account.

You will be required to fill out a Form 1099 if you paid more than $600 to consignors in one year. Send a copy of this form to the consignor, your state tax agency, and the IRS. Copy B of this form should be sent to the consignor by recipient by January 31 of the year following the end of the tax year, and Copy A should be filed with the IRS by February 28. If you file electronically, the due date is April 2.

Education

When you start a new business, you might need training to learn everything you need to know to run your business properly. You might take classes in accounting or bookkeeping, computer programs, or business management. You also might participate in seminars, online classes, and workshops to learn more about listing on online marketplaces and using social media. Expense and educational materials that further your business-related education are deductible.

Deductible education expenses include business-related books, newspapers, magazines, seminars (such as the Professional eBay Sellers Alliance), and conferences or conventions (such as eBay Live!). You must be able to prove to the IRS that these educational courses were necessary to help you further your business. Syllabuses, course schedules, certificates, and coursework all show how a particular class or seminar relates to your business. Keep receipts for all course fees, books purchased, and registration fees.

Inventory

Many online sales businesses maintain an inventory. You can deduct inventory costs from your business income as "cost of goods sold." Many expenses associated with your inventory can be deducted, including storage and shipping costs, and deductions for using part of your home to store or manufacture inventory. *Chapter 7 discusses how to manage your inventory, calculate its value, and keep accurate records.* Inventory left over at the end of the tax year is considered an asset and cannot be deducted from your income.

Employees

If you hire employees, rather than contract workers, you can deduct employee benefits, payroll expenses, pension plans, disability insurance, day care for employee's children, salaries to employees, unemployment taxes, and Medicare. Remember that you cannot claim yourself as an employee unless your business is structured as a corporation.

Having employees means complying with additional requirements, such as labor laws and safety regulations, and it also increases your bookkeeping and accounting work.

Travel

You can deduct the expenses of traveling away from home for your business. You are traveling away from home when you are away substantially longer than an ordinary workday and you need to sleep or rest to meet the demands of your work while away from home. Your home is not necessarily the house where you live. Your "tax home" is your main place of business, where you earn most of your income. Travel expenses apply to trips you take away from your tax home. Your tax home includes the entire city or general area in which your business or work is located.

Common deductible travel expenses are business trip airfare, lodging, meals on business trips, meals with customers, parking costs, and per-diem rates.

Travel expenses you can deduct

From *IRS Pub. 463*

IF YOU HAVE	THEN YOU CAN DEDUCT THE COST OF...
Transportation	Travel by airplane, train, bus, or car between your tax home and business destination. If you were provided with a ticket or you are riding free because of a frequent traveler or similar program, your cost is zero. If you travel by ship, see Luxury Water Travel and Cruise in Pub. 463·
Taxi, commuter bus, and airport limousine	Fares for these and other types of transportation that take you between the airport or station and your hotel, the hotel and the work location of your customers, your business meeting place or your temporary work location
Baggage and shipping	Sending baggage and sample or display material between your regular and temporary work locations

IF YOU HAVE	THEN YOU CAN DEDUCT THE COST OF...
Car	Operating and maintaining your car when traveling away from home on business. You can deduct actual expenses or the standard mileage rate, as well as business-related tolls and parking. If you rent a car while away from home on business, you can deduct only the business-use portion of the expenses.
Lodging and meals	Your lodging and meals if your business trip is overnight or long enough that you need to stop for sleep or rest to properly perform your duties. Meals include amounts spent for food, beverages, taxes, and related tips.
Cleaning	Dry cleaning and laundry
Telephone	Business calls while on your business trip; this includes business communicating by fax machine or other communication devices
Tips	Tips you pay for any expenses in this chart
Other	Other similar ordinary and necessary expenses related to your business travel. These expenses might include transportation to or from a business meal, public stenographer's fees, computer rental, and operating and maintaining a house trailer.

When you combine business with personal travel, you can deduct the percentage of your expenses equivalent to the portion of your trip that is business-related. You cannot deduct expenses such as meals for family members who are not directly involved in the business. When the purpose of the trip is primarily personal, but you do one or two business-related activities, you can deduct only the expenses related to the business activity. For example, if you have lunch with a business contact while on a vacation trip with your family, you can only deduct the cost of the business lunch.

Entertainment

Entertainment expenses can be deducted from your business income if they can be classified as "ordinary and necessary" expenses and if they pass one of two tests: the "directly related test" or the "associated test." Under the directly related test, the active conduct of your business must have been the main purpose of the combined business and entertainment, you engaged in business during the entertainment period, and you specifically expected to get income or some business benefit as a result. Even if the entertainment does not meet these requirements, it can meet the associated test if it occurred directly before or after a business discussion and was associated with the conduct of your business.

Expenses deductible as entertainment:

- Meal as a form of entertainment (can include cost of food, beverages, taxes, and tips, but you must be present at the meal)

- Trade association meetings (must be directly related to your business and necessary)

- Entertainment tickets (no more than the face value, cannot include any service charges)

Items that are not deductible:

- Club dues and membership fees (for business, pleasure, or recreation including country clubs, golf clubs, and airline clubs)

- Entertainment facilities

- Out-of-pocket expenses provided during entertainment at a facility

- Expenses for spouses

- Lavish or extravagant expenses (determined case-by-case)

- Gifts (unless they follow guidelines discussed earlier)

The IRS "50-percent limit" allows you to deduct only half of your entertainment expenses. In addition to the cost of meals and tickets, you can deduct half of:

- Taxes and tips relating to a business meal or entertainment activity

- Cover charges for admission to a nightclub

- Rent paid for a room in which you hold a dinner or cocktail party

- Amounts paid for parking at a sports arena

The 50-percent limit applies to meals and entertainment at your place of business as well as at restaurants and other outside locations. If you provide free entertainment or meals to the public, sell any type of meal or entertainment, or host a charitable sports event, then you are not subject to this limit. Detailed information about entertainment expenses can be found in *IRS Publication 463: Travel, Entertainment, Gift and Car Expenses* (**www. irs.gov/pub/irs-pdf/p463.pdf**).

Fees and licenses

You can deduct all kinds of fees and licenses related to your business from taxable income. These include fees paid to accountants, attorneys, bookkeeping services, customs, business credit-card providers, local and state licensing bureaus, and your homeowner's association (if you run your business in your home); licenses needed to start your business; membership fees to professional organizations; and Internet access fees. Keep accurate records of the money you spent for any fees and licenses for your business, all receipts, and copies of every license.

Finding Hidden Business Deductions

This chapter has given you an overview of the numerous expenses that can be deducted from your taxable income to reduce the amount you pay in taxes. Some of these expenses, such as the cost of acquiring inventory and buying packaging materials, are obvious. You might be able to keep even more of your money if you can identify additional "hidden business deductions" by re-evaluating your business expenses. In some cases, you have to be willing to make extra effort, such as writing your mileage in a notebook each time you make a trip to an office supply store.

Any deduction or expense you take should be well documented in your records and backed up with receipts and other solid evidence. Fabricating expenses, like hiding income, is unethical and could land you in serious trouble if you are selected for an audit. Hidden business deductions are legitimate expenses that the IRC allows you to deduct because they affect your bottom line.

Familiarity with the tax code, knowledge of basic accounting, and detailed, accurate records are all you need to search for hidden deductions. You might want to consult a tax accountant for expert advice on how to set up your books so you can take as many deductions as possible. The Internet is a good source of information; when you have a doubt or a question you usually can find the answer in a business publication or a tax blog. Always verify information with two or three reliable sources. Every online sales business is unique; only you can discover the deductions that apply to your particular activities.

Among the most commonly overlooked expenses are startup costs when you are preparing to launch your business. These can include fees for book-keeping and recordkeeping, incorporation or business registration, office equipment and furniture, inventory storage, office supplies, software, licensing, and consulting fees to attorneys or accountants.

Your day-to-day activities also can result in deductible expenses. When you drive your car to garage sales to look for merchandise, to the post office to ship packages, or to the store to buy office supplies, you can deduct mileage or expenses for business use of your car. If you use the Internet primarily for business, then Internet access fees qualify as business expenses. Are you paying extra for Wi-Fi connection when you are out on the road looking for bargains? Add those charges to your business expenses. Are you paint-ing the house where your home office is located? Part of that expense can be deducted as maintenance.

You can subtract depreciation each year for assets that last longer than one year, such as computers. Do not overlook assets, such as office chairs, fax machines, cell phones, and printers. You cannot depreciate an asset if you included its full cost in your business expenses when you bought it. You can depreciate a personal asset that you converted to business purposes.

Self-employed individuals are allowed to deduct 100 percent of their health insurance premiums on *Form 1040*. If you have employees, the health insurance premiums you pay for them are deductible. You also can deduct costs for business-related fire, theft, flood, liability, casualty, and inventory insurance.

Some of the travel expenses in the chart above are easy to overlook, such as the cost of dry cleaning your clothes during a business trip, tolls, tips, or the cost of shipping samples.

Your personal activities also can generate some "hidden deductions." When you do volunteer work for a charity, you can deduct travel expenses for the use of public transportation or your car, including tolls and parking. Keep receipts and tickets or a record of your mileage. You also can deduct the value of items you donate to charity, as long as you get a written receipt. Items worth more than $5,000 must be professionally appraised. You can get a deduction for costs associated with selling your home, for mortgage and home equity loan interest, and for certain types of education expenses. Remember that to claim many of these deductions the expenses must be itemized, and that you can only deduct the amount that exceeds 2 percent of your AGI.

CHAPTER 5

Business Use of Your Home

If you are operating your Internet sales business from your home, you could be eligible for a home-office tax deduction. If you rented or owned an office space or warehouse, your cost of doing business would include expenses, such as rent, utilities, taxes, telephone lines, maintenance, insurance, and security. The deduction for business use of your home allows you to deduct a certain amount from your business income to account for the fact that part of your home is really a business facility and the expenses for that part of your home are part of your cost of doing business. The IRS allows you to take deductions on the business portions of real estate, taxes, mortgage interest, rent, utilities, insurance, depreciation, painting, and repairs.

The home office deduction means a great deal to an online seller because it allows a significant reduction of taxable income. To qualify for the home-office deduction, you must use your home as your "principal place of business" or as a "place to meet or deal with your clients or customers in the normal course of your trade business." You qualify if you operate your online sale business out of your house. The amount you can deduct will depend on how much of your home you are using for your business.

The strict and detailed rules for calculating the deduction are explained in *IRS Publication 587: Business Use of Your Home* (**www.irs.gov/pub/irs-pdf/ p587.pdf**). The first year you take this deduction, you have to do a considerable amount of extra work to prepare your taxes. The following years are much easier because you have established the basic facts, and you know

what documents to keep on file and where to look for specific information. Tax preparation software takes you step-by-step through the process of calculating your deduction and does the math for you. You might want help from a tax accountant the first year to identify what you can deduct and establish the value of your home; you can follow the example of your first return to fill out future returns.

As with all tax matters, you will get the maximum allowable deduction only if you keep accurate records and file supporting receipts and documents. Receipts for maintenance and repairs, the purchase of replacement parts, utilities, HOA assessments, carpet cleaning, and pest control are all important because a portion of those costs can be deducted as business expenses. The IRS allows you to deduct more if your gross income is greater than your total business expenses than if you experience a business loss.

When selecting individuals for audit, the IRS is inclined to target taxpayers who take the home-office deduction because there are many opportunities for fabrication and abuse. You have nothing to worry about, however, if your deduction is legitimate, and you have hard evidence to back you up.

Compliance with Local Zoning Regulations

Before taking deductions for business use of your home, consider whether it is legal to operate a business in your house. Zoning laws in some counties do not allow businesses in residential areas, particularly if large numbers of deliveries are made to your house or you employ workers to pack or manufacture products there. Most zoning authorities will not care that you are quietly running your business from a computer in your spare room, but you could get into trouble if a neighbor reports you for disturbing the residential character of the neighborhood. You can avoid drawing undue attention to your activities by renting a mailbox at a UPS store to receive deliveries and storing inventory at a storage facility. These costs are fully deductible as business expenses.

How to Qualify

The IRS lists six different circumstances under which individuals can take the home business deduction. You must use part of your home for at least one of the following:

- "Exclusively and regularly as your principal place of business"

- "Exclusively and regularly as a place where you meet or deal with patients, clients, or customers in the normal course of your trade or business"

- "In the case of a separate structure which is not attached to your home, in connection with your trade or business"

- "On a regular basis for certain storage use"

- "For rental use"

- "As a day-care facility"

Before you can deduct expenses for the business use of your home, you must establish that your Internet sales activities can be considered a legitimate business and not a hobby or casual sales. *Chapter 1 discusses this distinction.*

You must use a specific area of your home only for your business. This does not have to be an entire room, but it must be separately identifiable as your work area. It does not have to be separated from the rest of the room by a partition. You must use your home office or workspace on a regular basis. Make sure it does not appear as though you only use this space occasionally or incidentally. There is an exception if you are storing inventory or samples for your business in part of your home — you still qualify if you use the storage area for personal activities. For example, you could store boxes of merchandise in your basement and still use it to watch TV. The storage area must be separately identifiable and suitable for storage, and your home must be your only fixed place of business.

If you conduct business at several locations, your home must be your principal place of business to qualify. This can be determined by calculating what percentage of your business activity is carried out at each location and each location's relative importance. Your home office will qualify as your principal place of business if you use it exclusively and regularly for managerial and administrative activities, such as billing customers, keeping books and records, ordering supplies, forwarding orders, or writing reports. You still can qualify if you have other people conduct your administrative or management activities at other locations, you occasionally conduct minimal administrative or management activities at a fixed location outside your home, or you have another location where you could do these activities, but you choose to do them at your home office.

You also can deduct business expenses if your business is in a separate structure from your home, such as a garage or studio, if you can prove that you use the space solely for business purposes. It does not have to be your principal place of business or a place that you meet customers, but it must be connected to your business in some way. An example of this would be storing inventory in a shed behind your house.

Figuring the Deduction

A self-employed business owner who files a *Schedule C (Form 1040) Profit or Loss from Business* can figure out the home office deduction using *Form 8829, Expenses for Business Use of Your Home*. A sample of *Form 8829* can be found below.

A partner, employee, or a taxpayer who files a *Schedule F (Form 1040) Profit or Loss From Farming* must use the *Worksheet to Figure the Deduction for Business Use of Your Home* found in *IRS Publication 587*.

Determining the business percentage of your home

Your business percentage is found by comparing the size of the section of your home you use for your business to the size of your home as a whole. You can use any method to do this, but the IRS gives two common examples of methods for determining your business percentage. If the rooms in your home are of similar size, and you use one or more entire rooms for business, you can divide the number of rooms you use for your business by the total number of rooms in your house. You also can measure the length and width of the area you use for your office or for storage, multiply them to find the area, and divide this number by the total area of your home. (The area of your home can be found on tax documents and title deeds.) This will give you the percentage of your home that is used for business. Suppose the area of your home is 1,400 square feet, and you use a bedroom for your office and a space in your garage for storage.

Total area of home	1,400 sq. ft.
Office in bedroom 10 ft. X 10 ft.	100 sq. ft.
Storage space in garage 5 ft. X 7 ft.	35 sq. ft.

Total space used for business	135 sq. ft.
Business portion of home	**9.64%**

IRS Form 8829: Business Use of Your Home

The following IRS form is what you would use to calculate the amount of money you could deduct from your home expenses for business reasons:

Form **8829**	Expenses for Business Use of Your Home	OMB No. 1545-0074
	☒ File only with Schedule C (Form 1040). Use a separate Form 8829 for each home you used for business during the year.	**2011**
Department of the Treasury Internal Revenue Service (99)	☒ See separate instructions.	Attachment Sequence No. **176**
Name(s) of proprietor(s)		Your social security number

Part I   Part of Your Home Used for Business

1	Area used regularly and exclusively for business, regularly for daycare, or for storage of inventory or product samples (see instructions)	1	
2	Total area of home	2	
3	Divide line 1 by line 2. Enter the result as a percentage	3	%

For daycare facilities not used exclusively for business, go to line 4. All others go to line 7.

4	Multiply days used for daycare during year by hours used per day	4		hr.
5	Total hours available for use during the year (365 days x 24 hours) (see instructions)	5		
6	Divide line 4 by line 5. Enter the result as a decimal amount . . .	6	.	
7	Business percentage. For daycare facilities not used exclusively for business, multiply line 6 by line 3 (enter the result as a percentage). All others, enter the amount from line 3 . . . . . ☒	7		%

Part II   Figure Your Allowable Deduction

8	Enter the amount from Schedule C, line 29, **plus** any gain derived from the business use of your home and shown on Schedule D or Form 4797, minus any loss from the trade or business not derived from the business use of your home and shown on Schedule D or Form 4797. See instructions . .	8

See instructions for columns (a) and (b) before completing lines 9–21.

		(a) Direct expenses	(b) Indirect expenses	
9	Casualty losses (see instructions).	9		
10	Deductible mortgage interest (see instructions)	10		
11	Real estate taxes (see instructions)	11		
12	Add lines 9, 10, and 11	12		
13	Multiply line 12, column (b) by line 7	13		
14	Add line 12, column (a) and line 13		14	
15	Subtract line 14 from line 8. If zero or less, enter -0-		15	
16	Excess mortgage interest (see instructions) .	16		
17	Insurance	17		
18	Rent	18		
19	Repairs and maintenance	19		
20	Utilities	20		
21	Other expenses (see instructions).	21		
22	Add lines 16 through 21	22		
23	Multiply line 22, column (b) by line 7	23		
24	Carryover of operating expenses from 2010 Form 8829, line 42 . .	24		
25	Add line 22 column (a), line 23, and line 24.		25	
26	Allowable operating expenses. Enter the **smaller** of line 15 or line 25		26	
27	Limit on excess casualty losses and depreciation. Subtract line 26 from line 15		27	
28	Excess casualty losses (see instructions)	28		
29	Depreciation of your home from line 41 below	29		
30	Carryover of excess casualty losses and depreciation from 2010 Form 8829, line 43	30		
31	Add lines 28 through 30		31	
32	Allowable excess casualty losses and depreciation. Enter the **smaller** of line 27 or line 31 . .		32	
33	Add lines 14, 26, and 32.		33	
34	Casualty loss portion, if any, from lines 14 and 32. Carry amount to **Form 4684** (see instructions)		34	
35	**Allowable expenses for business use of your home.** Subtract line 34 from line 33. Enter here and on Schedule C, line 30. If your home was used for more than one business, see instructions ☒		35	

Part III   Depreciation of Your Home

36	Enter the **smaller** of your home's adjusted basis or its fair market value (see instructions) . .	36	
37	Value of land included on line 36	37	
38	Basis of building. Subtract line 37 from line 36	38	
39	Business basis of building. Multiply line 38 by line 7.	39	
40	Depreciation percentage (see instructions).	40	%
41	Depreciation allowable (see instructions). Multiply line 39 by line 40. Enter here and on line 29 above	41	

Part IV   Carryover of Unallowed Expenses to 2012

42	Operating expenses. Subtract line 26 from line 25. If less than zero, enter -0-	42	
43	Excess casualty losses and depreciation. Subtract line 32 from line 31. If less than zero, enter -0-	43	

For Paperwork Reduction Act Notice, see your tax return instructions.	Cat. No. 13232M	Form **8829** (2011)

Deduction limit

If your business is not profitable, there is a limit to how much you can deduct. When the gross income from your business is greater than your total business expenses, you can deduct all of your home office expenses.

> **Gross income from home business use ≥ total business expense**
> **= you can deduct**

If your business income is not greater than your expenses, your deductions will be limited. To see how much you can deduct, subtract the business part of expenses you could deduct even if you did not use your home for business (mortgage interest, real estate taxes, and casualty and theft losses), plus your business expenses that do not relate to your use of the home, from your gross income. (Do not include your half of self-employment tax in the business expenses.) The remainder is how much you can deduct.

If your deductions exceed your limit, you are allowed to carry over these deductions to the next year. They will be subject to the deduction limit for that year.

Deducting Your Expenses

Some expenses related to your home can be deducted from your personal taxable income, even if you do not use your home for business. These include qualified mortgage interest, mortgage insurance premiums, real estate taxes, and casualty and theft losses. If you deduct expenses for the business use of your home, you must separate the business and personal portions of these deductions. The business percentage is recorded as a business expense, and the personal portion is still a deduction on your income tax return.

Other expenses such as depreciation, insurance, rent, and repairs can be deducted from business expenses only if you use your home for business.

The three types of home business expenses are: direct, indirect, and unrelated. Direct expenses relate only to the business part of your home and are deductible in full. Examples would be installing storage shelves only in the section of your home that houses your business or renovating a bedroom into an office. Indirect expenses are the general costs of maintaining your house and running your entire home. You can deduct a portion of these expenses equal to the percentage of your home used for business. Unrelated expenses relate only to the part of your home not used for business and are not deductible.

Repairs, such as patching walls and floors, painting, wallpapering, repairing roofs and gutters, and mending leaks, keep your home in good working order over its useful life and are deductible as business expenses. Improvements that add to the permanent value of the house, such as a kitchen makeover or new windows, are not deductible and must be depreciated instead. It is important to distinguish between permanent improvements, which are depreciated, and repairs, which are reported as business expenses. If repairs are part of an extensive remodeling project, the entire project is treated as an improvement.

Expenses for utilities and services, such as electricity, gas, trash removal, and cleaning services, are primarily personal expenses. However, if you use part of your home for business, you can deduct the business portion of these expenses. To calculate the deduction, multiply the amounts on these bills by the percentage of your home used for business.

Telephone lines

The basic local telephone service charge, including taxes, for the first telephone line into your home (i.e., landline) is a nondeductible personal expense. However, charges for business long-distance phone calls on that line, as well as the cost of a second (or third) line into your home used exclusively for business, are deductible business expenses. Do not include these expenses as a cost of using your home for business. Deduct these charges separately on the appropriate form or schedule. For example, if you file *Schedule C (Form 1040)*, deduct these expenses on line 25, Utilities (instead of line 30, Expenses for business use of your home).

When a cell phone is used entirely for business calls, you can deduct your cell phone bill as a business expense, along with activation fees, accessories, chargers, and batteries. The cost of the new phone can be depreciated over seven years. If you use your cell phone for both business and personal calls, you can deduct only the business portion of your cell phone bill. For example, if 60 percent of your phone calls are business calls, you can deduct 60 percent of your cell phone bill as a business expense. If you can get an itemized cell phone bill showing each call, keep it for your records in case of an IRS audit.

Depreciating Your Home

If you qualify to deduct expenses for business use of your home and you own the home, you also can take a deduction for depreciation. The IRS allows you to claim some of the loss every year for "the wear and tear on the part of your home used for business." Because your land retains its value even while your house deteriorates, you can claim this deduction only on the value of your house, not the land it stands on. The costs of clearing, grading, planting, and landscaping are usually all part of the cost of land and cannot be depreciated.

To calculate your depreciation deduction you need the following information:

- The month and year you started using your home for business

- The adjusted basis (cost of your home plus cost of any permanent improvements made) and fair market value of your home, excluding the value of the land

- The cost of any improvements before and after you began using the property for business

- The percentage of your home used for business

The adjusted basis of your home is generally its cost, plus the cost of any permanent improvements you made to it, minus any casualty losses or depreciation deducted in earlier tax years. A permanent improvement increases the value of property, adds to its life, or gives it a new or different use. Examples of improvements are replacing electric wiring or plumbing, adding a new roof or addition, paneling, or remodeling. Include only what you actually spent on the improvement; if you did the labor yourself, you cannot include the cost of your time, only the cost of materials you bought. Other costs that should be added to the basis of your property are settlement fees, closing costs and legal fees incurred in the process of buying the property, the cost of extending utility service lines to the property, and assessments by local government for improvements, such as sidewalks and sewer lines. You cannot include costs associated with obtaining a mortgage. Subtract any money that you received as compensation for an easement (public use of your property, such as for a sidewalk or utility pole). You must subtract the depreciation you have claimed on previous tax returns. If you have questions about determining the adjusted basis of your property, you can find answers in *IRS Publication 946: How to Depreciate Property* (**www.irs.gov/pub/irs-pdf/p946.pdf**).

To determine the value of your land, find out from your original bill of sale how much you paid for your land and how much you paid for your building. If the bill of sale does not separate the cost of land and building, then look up your county property tax records, and use the values assigned by your county assessor. Divide the value of the land by the total value of the property. That will tell you what percentage of your adjusted basis or FMV should be assigned to your land. Multiply this percentage times the adjusted basis of your home to determine how much you must subtract for land.

Calculating your basis in your house and your land

You bought your house for $180,000. The purchase contract does not specify how much you paid for the house and how you paid for the land.

The latest real estate tax assessment on the property was based on an assessed value of $130,000, of which $106,000 was for the house and $24,000 was for the land.

You can allocate 82 percent ($106,000 ÷ $130,000) of the purchase price to the house and 18 percent ($24,000 ÷ $130,000) of the purchase price to the land.

Your basis in the house is $147,600 (82 percent of $180,000), and your basis in the land is $32,400 (18 percent of $180,000).

If you began using your home for business before 2010, continue using the same depreciation method you have used in past years. If you began using your home for business for the first time in 2010, depreciate the business part of your home as nonresidential real property under the modified accelerated cost recovery system (MACRS). MACRS assigns a lifespan of 39 years to your home and depreciates it using the straight-line method — each year you can subtract $1/39$th (2.56 percent) of your adjusted basis or FMV (whichever is smaller on the date when you begin to use your home for business).

Figure the part of the cost of your home that can be depreciated (depreciable basis) by multiplying the business percentage of your home by the smaller of the following:

- The adjusted basis of your home (excluding land) on the date you began using your home for business

- The fair market value of your home (excluding land) on the date you began using your home for business

If this is your first year using your home for business, select the month you started your business from this table to find the appropriate percentage to use.

MACRS Percentage Table for 39-Year Nonresidential Real Property

From *IRS Publication 587*

MONTH FIRST USED FOR BUSINESS	PERCENTAGE TO USE
1	2.46%
2	2.25%
3	2.03%
4	1.82%
5	1.61%
6	1.39%
7	1.18%
8	0.96%
9	0.75%
10	0.54%
11	0.32%
12	0.11%

For more information on MACRS and other methods of depreciation, see *IRS Publication 946: How to Depreciate Property* (**www.irs.gov/pub/irs-pdf/p946.pdf**).

If you made any permanent improvements only to the home office portion of your home, you can deduct depreciation for those improvements. A permanent improvement is anything that increases the value of your property, such as new wiring, roofing, or remodeling. Use this simple formula:

$$\frac{\text{Cost of improvements X business-use percentage}}{\text{Percentage recovery period (usually 39 years)}}$$

Most deductions will be listed on *Form 1040*. If you are self-employed and file a *Schedule C*, you will need to attach a completed Form *8829: Expenses for Business Use of Your Home* (**www.irs.gov/pub/irs-pdf/f8829.pdf**). If you are deducting your mortgage interest, real estate taxes, or casualty losses, then you will be required to fill out additional forms. Tax preparation software automatically determines which forms you need and fills them out as you go along. The instructions for *Form 1040* will tell you when you need additional forms if you are doing your taxes manually.

Making the Most of Your Home-Office Deductions

You can maximize your home office deductions by being aware of all the possible expenses that could be deducted and keeping receipts and accurate records. It is easy to overlook the cost of new light bulbs or a carpet cleaning service, but every expense adds up. Study *IRS Publication 587: Business Use of Your Home* (**www.irs.gov/pub/irs-pdf/p587.pdf**), and read articles and blogs on the subject to get some ideas.

Remember that you can lower taxable income for the year by being proactive and paying for planned repairs and maintenance before the end of the tax year. It is always a good idea to keep your property well maintained. Regular inspections and repairs contribute to energy efficiency and increase the value of your home when you eventually sell it. Knowing that a portion of these costs can be deducted as business expenses is an incentive to go ahead and spend the money. Of course, expenses paid for this year cannot be deducted on next year's tax return, even if the services are performed over a period of several months.

Increase the portion of your home expenses that you can deduct by expanding the area devoted to business in your home. If you have a spare bedroom, use the whole room as your office instead of just a desk or a corner. Remember that the space must be used exclusively for business and used on a regular basis to be eligible.

CHAPTER 6

More Deductions

P revious chapters have covered deductions that are available to most sole proprietors and home-based businesses. You may qualify to reduce your taxable business income even further using deductions that apply only in certain circumstances or to certain types of businesses. Your personal circumstances also may qualify for certain deductions or credits on your personal income tax — for example, credits for dependent care or for adopting a child. Some of these credits and deduction only may be available to you in a particular tax year.

The U.S. government uses tax incentives to stimulate business and consumer spending, support home ownership, encourage energy efficiency, and assist with recovery after a natural disaster. These opportunities change from year to year. Tax preparation software is programmed to ask you questions that will identify whether you qualify for these incentives, but do not wait until the end of the tax year to learn about them. You might decide to invest in a vehicle or an energy-efficient appliance during the year if you know you will reap a tax benefit. Some of the business activities you were planning, such as remodeling or purchasing new equipment, could become tax breaks if you execute them according to IRS rules. You can learn about tax incentives and new developments by reading business journals and websites and by subscribing to the IRS e-News services (**www.irs.gov/newsroom/content/0,,id=103381,00.html**). If you think you might be a candidate for a big tax break this year, consult a tax accountant or financial planner who can help you map out a strategy.

The strategies in this chapter are not fabrications or loopholes. They are legitimate ways in which you might be able to reap additional tax benefits from your existing circumstances.

Phantom Losses

A phantom loss is a business loss that is incurred legitimately on paper without actually spending or losing any money, such as depreciation of an asset that has been converted from personal to business use. Are you using furniture, computers, or equipment for your business that used to belong to you or a family member? You can calculate the value of the item when you put it into use, and record it as either a business expense or a capital expense to be depreciated. Do you have items in your inventory that you cannot sell because they are outdated or damaged? Gather evidence that their value has decreased, or destroy them, and write them off.

Depreciation

Are you depreciating your computer, fax machine, office furniture, or the trailer you use to haul your merchandise? Any income-producing property that has a useful life of more than one year potentially can be depreciated. For more information, read the IRS publication *A Brief Overview of Depreciation* (**www.irs.gov/businesses/small/article/0,,id=137026,00.html**).

Alternative Motor Vehicle Credit (Form 8910)

Qualifying alternative fuel vehicles (AFVs) purchased or placed into service between January 1, 2005, and December 31, 2010, might be eligible for a federal income tax credit of up to $4,000. The credit is available for certain new vehicles purchased and placed in service for business use during the tax year. There are five components to this credit:

1. **Qualified hybrid vehicles:** Hybrid vehicles are a combination of gasoline and electric engines. These vehicles have drive trains powered by both internal combustion engines and rechargeable batteries.

2. **Qualified fuel-cell vehicles:** A qualified fuel-cell motor vehicle is a vehicle that is propelled by power derived from one or more cells that convert chemical energy directly into electricity.

3. **Qualified alternative-fuel motor vehicles (QAFMV) and heavy hybrids:** For alternative fueled light and heavy-duty vehicles to meet the requirements of QAFMV, the vehicles may be either new, original equipment installation vehicles, or prior use vehicles that are converted to use an alternative fuel by an aftermarket installer. Qualified alternative fuel includes compressed natural gas, liquefied natural gas, liquefied petroleum gas (propane), and hydrogen. The vehicles also may operate on certain mixed fuels such as liquefied propane gas or liquefied natural gas and gasoline.

4. **Advanced lean-burn technology vehicles:** Advanced lean-burn vehicles are passenger cars or light trucks with an internal combustion engine designed to operate primarily using more air than is necessary for complete combustion of the fuel. The vehicles must incorporate direct-fuel-injection technology and achieve at least 125 percent of the 2002 model year city fuel economy rating.

5. **Plug-in conversion kits:** This is a tax credit for up to 10 percent of the cost of a kit that converts a fuel-burning vehicle to a qualified plug-in electric drive motor vehicle, to a maximum of $4,000. The credit does not apply to conversions made after December 31, 2011.

Year-End Tax Deductions

The tax year is ending, and you realize that your taxable income is higher than you expected. Look for ways to reduce your income or increase your deductible expenses before the end of the year.

Spend money to save money

Increase your business expenses by investing in a vehicle or purchasing a new phone before the end of the year. Pay in advance for a service contract. Purchase solar energy panels or an energy-efficient appliance for your home. Remember that you will not be able to deduct those expenses from next year's taxable income, and make better plans for next year.

Contribute to a traditional IRA

You can defer taxes on up to $5,000 ($6,000 if you are over 50) of your income by putting it in a traditional IRA and saving for retirement. You and your spouse can each contribute to an IRA, as long as you have enough combined earned income. *Chapter 12 discusses this in more detail.*

Donate to a charity

Get a tax deduction by donating cash or goods to a charity. The donation can be made from your business or your personal income. The donation must be made to a qualified charitable organization and cannot go to any individual or political organization. To claim a deduction for contributions of cash or property equaling $250 or more you must have a bank record, payroll deduction records, or a written acknowledgment from the qualified organization showing the amount of the cash and a description of any property contributed, and whether the organization provided any goods or services in exchange for the gift. One document may satisfy both the written communication requirement for monetary gifts and the written acknowledgment requirement for all contributions of $250 or more. For text-message donations, a telephone bill will meet the recordkeeping requirement if it shows the name of the receiving organization, the date of the contribution, and the amount given.

If your total deduction for all noncash contributions for the year is more than $500, then you must complete and attach *IRS Form 8283, Noncash Charitable Contributions*, to your return. Taxpayers donating an item or a group of similar items valued at more than $5,000 also must complete *Section B* of *Form 8283*, which generally requires an appraisal by a qualified appraiser.

Donations of stock or other noncash property usually are valued at the fair market value (FMV) of the property. However, if you are a dealer and you are donating a collectible from your inventory, its value is equal only to its inventory cost and not to what it might bring on the market. Clothing and household items generally must be in good used condition or better to be deductible. Special rules apply to vehicle donations. Be wary of making a vehicle donation because you might get little credit for it, and it must be properly documented.

For more information on charitable contributions, refer to *Form 8283, Noncash Charitable Contributions* (**www.irs.gov/pub/irs-pdf/f8283.pdf**) and its instructions, as well as *Publication 526, Charitable Contributions* (**www.irs.gov/pub/irs-pdf/p526.pdf**) For information on determining value, refer to *Publication 561, Determining the Value of Donated Property* (**www.irs.gov/pub/irs-pdf/p561.pdf**).

Section 179 deduction

Are you planning to buy a vehicle, machinery, equipment, or software for your business? Ordinarily, if you buy equipment, machinery, or a vehicle for your business, it is treated as a capital expense, and you gradually deduct depreciation year-by-year. *Section 179* of the IRC offers an incentive to stimulate business spending by allowing businesses to deduct up to $500,000 (2011) of the price of qualifying equipment and/or software from their gross incomes for the year in which the purchase is made. If you buy (or lease) qualifying equipment worth less than $500,000, then you can deduct the full purchase price from your gross income for that year. The equipment can be bought and placed into service any time during the tax year. The deduction cannot exceed your taxable business income. If you do not have taxable income in the year you purchase the equipment, you can use the "100% Bonus Depreciation" implemented by the Tax Relief Act of 2010 and carry forward the deduction to another tax year. The deduction is phased out for businesses that purchase more than $2 million worth of equipment. The property must have been acquired for business use.

Purchases eligible for the deduction include:

- Equipment (machines, etc) purchased for business use

- Tangible personal property used in business

- Business vehicles with a gross vehicle weight in excess of 6,000 pounds

- Computers

- Computer software (including "off-the-shelf" software, described below)

- Office furniture

- Office equipment

- Property attached to your building that is not a structural component of the building (i.e.: a printing press, large manufacturing tools, and equipment)

- Partial business use (equipment that is purchased for business use and personal use — generally, your deduction will be based on the percentage of time you use the equipment for business purposes)

Off-the-shelf computer software

The IRS defines off-the-shelf computer software as "computer software that is readily available for purchase by the general public, is subject to a nonexclusive license, and has not been substantially modified. It includes any program designed to cause a computer to perform a desired function. However, a database or similar item is not considered computer software unless it is in the public domain and is incidental to the operation of otherwise qualifying software." Off-the-shelf software is any program that you buy ready to use, such as QuickBooks, Microsoft Office 2010, and antivirus software programs.

You can also deduct the cost of energy property, which includes:

a. Equipment that uses solar energy to generate electricity, to heat or cool a structure, to provide hot water for use in a structure, or to provide solar process heat, except for equipment used to generate energy to heat a swimming pool

b. Equipment placed in service after December 31, 2005, and before January 1, 2017, that uses solar energy to illuminate the inside of a structure using fiber-optic distributed sunlight

c. Equipment used to produce, distribute, or use energy derived from a geothermal deposit. For electricity generated by geothermal power, this includes equipment up to (but not including) the electrical transmission stage.

d. Qualified fuel-cell property or qualified microturbine property placed in service after December 31, 2005, and before January 1, 2017

Vehicles

In the past, *Section 179* was sometimes referred to as the "Hummer Tax Loophole" because it allowed small business owners to purchase SUVs and write them off as business expenses. The IRS has now modified the requirements for vehicles. You cannot elect to expense more than $25,000 of the cost of any heavy sport utility vehicle (SUV) and certain other vehicles placed in service during the tax year. This rule applies to any four-wheeled vehicle primarily designed or used to carry passengers over public streets, roads, or highways, that is rated at more than 6,000 pounds gross vehicle weight and not more than 14,000 pounds gross vehicle weight. However, the $25,000 limit does not apply to any vehicle:

- Designed to seat more than nine passengers behind the driver's seat

- Equipped with a cargo area (either open or enclosed by a cap) of at least 6 feet in interior length that is not readily accessible from the passenger compartment

- That has an integral enclosure fully enclosing the driver compartment and load carrying device, does not have seating rearward of the driver's seat, and has no body section protruding more than 30 inches ahead of the leading edge of the windshield

Vehicles can be new or used. The vehicle can be financed with certain leases and loans or bought outright. The vehicle in question must be used for business at least 50 percent of the time, and these depreciation limits are reduced by the corresponding percentage of personal use if the vehicle is used for business less than 100 percent of the time. Suppose you use a van mostly for business, but drive it to drop your children off at school and to the grocery store. The miles you drive to school and the grocery store are about 30 percent of the total miles you drive the van, so your business use is only 70 percent. You can only depreciate the vehicle up to a limit of $17,500, or 70 percent of $25,000.

Homeowner Credits and Exemptions

Various tax credits are available to homeowners who pay for energy-efficient improvements on their homes. A tax credit means that you are reimbursed for part of the cost by subtracting it from your income tax.

Energy efficiency

Energy-efficient windows, doors, and skylights. Under the Tax Relief, Unemployment Insurance Reauthorization, and Job Creation Act of 2010, homeowners may claim a tax credit for the purchase of energy-efficient windows, doors, and skylights. Homeowners may receive a tax credit equal to 10 percent of the product cost (installation may not be included) up to $200 for eligible windows and skylights and $500 for eligible doors. To be eligible for the credit, windows, doors, and skylight must meet ENERGY STAR program requirements, be installed in a taxpayer's primary residence, and be installed by December 31, 2011.

Homeowners may receive no more than $500 total for all energy efficiency tax credits. These caps are also the new "lifetime limits" for the taxable years of 2006 to 2011. Homeowners should save all available documentation, such as purchase receipts, ENERGY STAR labels, and manufacturers' certification statements.

Residential Energy Property Credit (Section 1121). The American Recovery and Reinvestment Act provides tax incentives for individuals to invest in energy-efficient products. The Residential Energy Property Credit gives energy tax credits to homeowners who make energy efficient improvements to their existing homes. The credit is equal to 30 percent of the cost of all qualifying improvements, with a maximum credit limit of $1,500. The credit applies to improvements such as adding insulation, energy-efficient exterior windows, and energy-efficient heating and air conditioning systems.

Residential Energy Efficient Property Credit (Section 1122). This non-refundable energy tax credit will help individual taxpayers pay for qualified residential alternative energy equipment, such as solar hot water heaters, geothermal heat pumps, and wind turbines, by allowing for a credit equal to 30 percent of the cost of qualified property.

Disaster recovery

The National Disaster Relief Act of 2008 provides tax relief for victims of federally declared disasters occurring after December 31, 2007, and before January 1, 2010. To qualify, a loss must be attributable to a federally declared disaster and occur in an area determined by the President to warrant federal assistance. Legislation extending the provisions to disasters occurring after January 1, 2010, has been proposed but has not yet been signed into law. If you live in a federal disaster area, check with the IRS to see what help might be available. A federal disaster area is an area that has been designated by the President as officially qualified to receive emergency governmental aid because of a catastrophe, such as an earthquake, tornado, hurricane, flood, or forest fire.

Tax-free capital gains from the sale of your main home

Qualified homeowners can claim the first $250,000 of capital gain on the sale of their homes tax-free, and married couples filing jointly can claim $500,000. You are eligible for the exclusion if you have owned and used your home as your main home for a period aggregating at least two years out of the five years before its sale. Generally, you are not eligible for the exclusion if you excluded the gain from the sale of another home during the two-year period before the sale of your home. Military, foreign service, and intelligence personnel on qualified official extended duty can suspend this five-year period for up to ten years. Exceptions to the two-year rule allow you to exclude at least part of your capital gain if you sold your house because the location of your job changed, because of health concerns, or for some other unforeseen circumstance. You cannot deduct a loss from the sale of your main home. For more information, refer to *IRS Publication 523: Selling Your Home* (**www.irs.gov/publications/p523/index.html**).

Mortgage interest

If you pay interest on a mortgage or a home equity loan, it is deductible from your personal income tax as an itemized expense, like medical expenses and charitable donations. Fill out *Schedule A* to see if your itemized deductions exceed your standard deduction. If so, you will save more money on your taxes by itemizing.

Employer deductions

You may be eligible for certain tax deductions if you have employees (not independent contractors) working for you. These include:

Credit for employer-provided childcare facilities and services (Form 8882). This credit applies to the qualified expenses you paid for employee childcare and qualified expenses you paid for childcare resource and referral services. The credit cannot exceed $150,000 for the year.

Credit for small employer pension plan startup costs (Form 8881). This credit applies to pension plan startup costs of a new qualified defined benefit or defined contribution plan (including a 401(k) plan), SIMPLE plan, or simplified employee pension. The 50-percent credit applies to the first $1,000 in administrative expenses over the first three years to set up an employer pension plan and is limited to $500 per year. For more information, see *Publication 560, Retirement Plans for Small Business (SEP, Simple, and Qualified Plans.*

Credit for small employer health insurance premiums (Form 8941). This credit applies to the cost of certain health insurance coverage you provide to certain employees.

Credit for employer differential wage payments (Form 8932). This credit provides certain small businesses with an incentive to continue to pay wages to an employee performing services on active duty in the uniformed services of the United States for a period of more than 30 days.

Work opportunity credit (Form 5884). This credit provides businesses with an incentive to hire individuals from targeted groups that have a particularly high unemployment rate or other special employment needs. The Instructions for Form 5884 contain a list of targeted groups, such as unemployed veterans, qualified ex-felons, and welfare recipients. The list changes from year to year as certain targeted designations expire.

Empowerment zone and renewal community employment credit (Form 8844). You may qualify for this credit if you have employees and are engaged in a business in an empowerment zone for which the credit is available. Empowerment zones are certain distressed urban and rural areas designated by the U.S. Department of Agriculture (USDA) and Housing and Urban Development (HUD) to receive tax credits and other incentives. The Instructions for Form 8844 list the current empowerment zones.

CHAPTER 7

How to Value Your Inventory for Taxes

Most Internet sales businesses, except for those that sell items shipped directly to customers from a manufacturer or supplier, maintain an inventory. Your inventory is all the items you have in stock for sale online, along with any raw goods or materials to be used in manufacturing items for sale. When you calculate the profit (or loss) from your online sales business for your income tax return, you must subtract the cost of the goods you sold from your gross income.

If your online sales business buys and resells large quantities of the same item, or if you are buying items wholesale from a manufacturer or supplier, determining the cost of your inventory is simple: the wholesale price plus the cost of shipping the items to you and storing them. Many online sellers, however, deal in collectibles, used items, antiques, handmade goods, and one-of-a-kind items. You might be selling items acquired from thrift stores, garage sales, and flea markets; personal items that you bought a long time ago; books and clothes that were given to you by friends and family members; and even items that you found in your grandmother's attic. Each of these categories presents its own challenges. Items that you held for personal use before selling are treated differently from items that you bought specifically to resell. The profit from selling an antique that was in your family for years might be treated as a capital gain rather than business income. Antiques that you purchase for the purpose of reselling them, however, are treated as merchandise, and the profit from the sales is taxed as business income.

It might be difficult to accurately determine the value of a collectible or a unique item. Your cost basis is what you paid to acquire the item, including freight and insurance, and it may differ considerably from the value of that item on the market.

Cost of Goods Sold

If your business manufactures products or purchases them for resale, you generally must value inventory at the beginning and end of each tax year to determine your cost of goods sold. The difference between your gross receipts for the items you sell and your cost of goods sold, minus any returns, is your business income from your online sales activities. You then subtract your business expenses (cost of doing business) from that business income to determine your net income for the year.

Some expenses related to your inventory, such as freight, storage, and insurance, may be included in figuring the cost of goods sold. Cost of goods sold is deducted from your gross receipts along with your business expenses to figure your gross profit for the year. If you include an expense in the cost of goods sold, you cannot deduct it again as a business expense. These types of expenses contribute to the cost of goods sold.

- The cost of products or raw materials, including freight
- Storage

- Direct labor costs (including contributions to pensions or annuity plans) for workers who produce the products
- Factory overhead

Are you a multi-million dollar seller?

Sellers who have realized more than $10 million in sales during the three preceding tax years are subject to uniform capitalization rules (UNICAP), which means they must include many indirect costs associated with purchase and production of inventory in the cost of goods sold rather than deducting them as business expenses. These indirect costs include purchasing costs, handling, warehousing, security, cost accounting, data processing, production coordination, bidding costs, engineering and design, employee benefit expenses, quality control, rent, utilities, tools and equipment, production bonuses, and insurance. More information can be found in the IRS publication, *Cost Segregation Audit Technique Guide — Chapter 6.1 Uniform Capitalization* (**www.irs.gov/businesses/article/0,,id=134361,00.html**).

Your accounting system should include a ledger or spreadsheet to record each item in your inventory, including the date you acquired it, what you paid for it, the cost of having it shipped to you (if any), including insurance and storage, and any expenses associated with cleaning or repairing it to make it ready for resale. *Chapter 2 describes how to set up a record of your inventory.* If you are conscientious about keeping your inventory records accurate and up-to-date, it will take only minutes to calculate your cost of goods sold at the end of the year.

At any given moment, some of your goods may be in transit, on order but not yet shipped, or in the process of being returned. These items must be accounted for in your cost of goods sold. On the last day of the tax year, your inventory should include:

- Merchandise you have purchased and for which title has passed to you, including merchandise in transit. The terms of purchase generally indicate when title passes, for example free on board (FOB), free along side (FAS), or cost, insurance and freight (CIF).

- Goods that are under contract for sale, but that you have not yet applied to the contract

- Goods that you own and have consigned out to another location (You have consigned the goods but have not sold them or transferred ownership.)

- Goods that are held for sale at showrooms, or other points of sale outside your normal place of business

- If you sell by mail and your sales terms are cash on delivery (COD), you should keep the merchandise in your inventory until payment is received from the buyer.

Merchandise that should not be included in your inventory includes:

- Goods that have been sold, and title has passed to the buyer

- Goods you are holding on consignment for someone else

- Goods you have ordered for future delivery, but for which you do not yet have title

According to the Universal Commercial Code (UCC), the title passes in a physical auction when the auctioneer's gavel comes down. Online marketplaces typically specify when title passes in their terms of service policies. Unless you make other arrangements, title passes to the buyer as soon as the payment clears.

You can deduct the cost of damaged, worthless, or obsolete items from the value of your closing inventory at the end of the tax year. This will increase your cost of goods sold. For damaged inventory, report its estimated value.

If you subtract the cost of worthless inventory, you must provide evidence that it was destroyed. For obsolete inventory, you must show evidence of its decrease in value. You can find more information about valuing your inventory in IRS *Publication 538: Accounting Periods and Methods* (**www.irs.gov/pub/irs-pdf/p538.pdf**).

Methods for Valuing Inventory

The type of items you sell will determine the method you use to value your inventory. Unique items and collectibles each must be listed separately using the specific identification method. The cost method tracks the cost of acquiring each item. If you are buying quantities of manufactured items wholesale that rotate in and out of your storage, you might use the LIFO (last in, first out) method or the FIFO (first in, first out) method. These methods are explained below. If you are producing the items yourself, you will need to allocate production expenses and the cost of raw materials to each item.

Cost method

The cost method, also known as the perpetual inventory method, tracks the purchase price of each item in your inventory, plus any additional costs, such as shipping, storage, and repair. You must keep your inventory records up-to-date and regularly reconcile them with the items in stock.

First in, first out (FIFO)

The first in, first out method assumes the items you have purchased or produced first are the first items you sold, consumed, or otherwise disposed of. The items in inventory at the end of the tax year are matched with the costs of items of the same type that you most recently purchased or produced.

Last in, first out (LIFO)

The last in, first out method assumes the items of inventory you purchased or produced last are sold or removed from inventory first. Items included in closing inventory are considered to be from the opening inventory in the order of acquisition and acquired in that tax year. The rules for using the LIFO method are complex. Two common methods are used to price LIFO inventories: the dollar-value method and the simplified dollar-value method.

- **Dollar-value method.** Under the dollar-value method of pricing LIFO inventories, goods and products must be grouped into one or more pools (classes of items), depending on the kinds of goods or products in the inventories.

- **Simplified dollar-value method.** Under this method, you establish multiple inventory pools in general categories from appropriate government price indexes. You then use changes in the price index to estimate the annual change in price for inventory items in the pools. An eligible small business (average annual gross receipts of $5 million or less for the three preceding tax years) can elect this method.

To adopt the LIFO method file *Form 970, Application To Use LIFO Inventory Method* (**www.irs.gov/pub/irs-pdf/f970.pdf**). You must notify the IRS if you decide to change your method of valuing inventory.

Retail Method

If you regularly price your items for resale by marking them up a specific percentage, you can use the retail method to calculate your cost of goods sold. Multiply your total sales by the retail markup percentage, and subtract that amount from the total sales to get the cost of goods sold. You must inform the IRS on your tax return that you are using this method.

Garage Sales, Thrift Stores, Flea Markets, and Auctions

You should have a receipt and/or invoice to document that cost of each item in your inventory ledger. Ideally, you should get a formal written receipt for each item you purchase. This might not be possible when you buy half a dozen items at a garage sale or a box of assorted junk at a flea market or thrift store. In these situations, carry a notebook with you, write out your own receipt with the date, and ask the seller to sign it. If this is not feasible, keep a written record of where you bought something, the date, and how much you paid. If you are selected for an audit, such records show that you are treating your online sales as a business. If you have no record that you paid anything for an item, you will not be able to deduct the cost of goods sold. For your own purposes, you cannot track your profits from your business if you do not know how much you spent acquiring the items you sell.

When you place an item in your inventory, assign it a unique inventory number, and record it in your ledger. Tag each item with its inventory number and keep your inventory organized so you can see at a glance when an item has been removed. At the end of the tax year, check your items against your inventory ledger to confirm they are still part of your inventory. It is easy to misplace items or forget to record them as sold when you are busy or in a hurry.

What if you paid $30 for an item at a garage sale, and then you got home and found it is selling online for $5 or $6? If it is still sitting in your inventory at the end of the tax year, use the lower of cost or market method to determine its value. Compare its market value on the inventory date with its cost, and use the lower value as its inventory value. This method applies both to items you purchase and to the materials you purchase to make the items you sell along with indirect production costs. You can determine an item's market value by looking at prices for similar items on online marketplaces.

Personal Items and Collectibles

Almost everything you own and use for personal purposes, pleasure, or investment is a capital asset. Your capital assets include:

Household furnishings

A car used for pleasure or commuting

Coin or stamp collections

Gems and jewelry

Gold, silver, or any other metal

When you sell a capital asset, the difference between the amount you sell it for and your basis — which is usually what you paid for it — is a capital gain or a capital loss. When you sell an item that you bought and used for a while, such as a set of golf clubs or children's clothing, you probably will receive only a fraction of what you paid for. The difference between the item's original cost and what you sold it for is considered a personal loss and cannot be deducted from your taxable income. You do not need to report personal losses on your tax return.

If you make a profit selling a valuable collectible, such as a painting you bought years ago or your coin collection, the profit is considered a capital gain and is taxed at the lower capital gains rate. The tax rates that apply to net capital gains are generally lower than the tax rates that apply to other income. For 2010, the maximum capital gains rate for most people was 15 percent. Gains on the sales of collectibles are taxed at 28 percent for those in income tax brackets of 28 percent and above. *Schedule D* defines collectibles as "works of art, rugs, antiques, precious metals (such as gold, silver, and platinum bullion), gems, stamps, coins, and certain other tangible property."

Capital gains and losses are classified as long-term or short-term, depending on how long you hold the property before you sell it. If you hold it more than one year, your capital gain or loss is long term. If you hold it one year or less, your capital gain or loss is short term.

Capital gains and losses are reported on *Schedule D, Capital Gains and Losses* (**www.irs.gov/pub/irs-pdf/f1040sd.pdf**) and then transferred to line 13 of *Form 1040*.

For more information about reporting capital gains and losses, see the *Schedule D instruction; Publication 550: Investment Income and Expenses* (**www.irs.gov/pub/irs-pdf/p550.pdf**) or *Publication 17: Your Federal Income Tax* (**www.irs.gov/pub/irs-pdf/p17.pdf**).

Inherited items and gifts

To calculate your capital gain when you sell an item that was given to you or that you inherited, you must first determine your basis, or the value of the item when it is in your possession. When you inherit an item, your basis is the fair market value (FMV) of the property on the date of the individual's death. If the item was a gift, it is the FMV on the date the item was given to you.

CHAPTER 8

Self-Employment Taxes

S elf-employment taxes are reported and paid on your federal income tax return, but they are not the same as federal income tax. They are the amounts you contribute to Social Security and Medicare during your working years so you can receive benefits when you reach retirement age. Employment taxes finance Social Security's *Old-Age, Survivors, and Disability Insurance* (OASDI) program and Medicare's *Hospital Insurance* (HI) program. The self-employment tax rate is a percentage of your net self-employment earnings set by law.

When you work for an employer, employment taxes are automatically deducted from your paycheck. You pay half, and your employer pays the other half. The employer collects the taxes and submits the money to the IRS, which transfers it to the Social Security Administration (SSA). When you work for yourself, you are responsible for paying both your portion and the employer's portion. The amount you pay is set by law: 10.4 percent (in 2011) of your net earnings up to $106,800 for Social Security and 2.9

percent of all earnings for Medicare. This means you will pay 13.3 percent of your 2011 net earnings to the federal government. The taxes are calculated based on 91.9 percent of your net earnings. The other 8.1 percent is subtracted before the calculation to account for the half that is usually paid by the employer from your net earnings.

Self-employment tax is calculated based on your adjusted net earnings.

Net earnings	Net income minus business expenses	$25,000.00
MINUS	8.1% of net earnings	$2,025.00
Adjusted net earnings		$22,975.00
Self-employment Tax	13.3% of adjusted net earnings	$3,055.68

You also can deduct half of your Social Security tax on *IRS Form 1040*. The deduction must be taken from your gross income in determining your adjusted gross income; it cannot be an itemized deduction and must not be listed on your *Schedule C: Profit or Loss from Business*.

2011 Social Security tax holiday temporarily lowers rates

To put more spending money in the wallets of U.S. workers, Congress temporarily reduced of the amount of Social Security tax they must pay. For 2011 only, employees will pay 4.2 percent of their net earnings instead of the normal 6.2 percent. Employers still pay the full 6.2 percent tax rate. That makes the Social Security tax rate for self-employed persons 10.4 percent instead of 12.4 percent, and the total amount of self-employment tax 13.3 percent for 2011.

Who Pays Self-Employment Tax

The IRS considers you a self-employed individual if you are "a sole proprietor (including an independent contractor), a partner in a partnership, including a member of a multi-member limited liability company (LLC), or are otherwise in business for yourself." (A "sole proprietor" also refers to members of a husband-and-wife qualified joint venture.) You usually must pay self-employment tax if you had net earnings from self-employment of $400 or more during the tax year.

If you are working for an employer and operating your online sales business on the side, your employer will withhold Social Security and Medicare tax from your paycheck, and you are only responsible for paying self-employment taxes on the income from your sales. Social Security tax is only paid on the first $106,800 of your wages and net earnings (maximum wage base), so the most you will pay in 2011 is $11,107.20 (10.4 percent). The maximum wage base is determined every year, so check the IRS and SSA websites each year for the current maximum. If you work at a job where you are paid $106,800 or more, you will not need to pay any Social Security tax out of your online sales income.

There is no cap on income for Medicare taxes; you will continue to pay 2.9 percent of your earned income no matter how much you make. Beginning in 2013, an additional HI tax of 0.9 percent is assessed on earned income exceeding $200,000 for individuals and $250,000 for married couples filing jointly.

Certain types of income are not subject to self-employment tax:

- Dividends from shares of stock and interest on bonds, unless you receive them as a dealer in stocks and securities

- Interest from loans, unless your business is lending money

- Rentals from real estate, unless you are a real estate dealer or regularly provide services mostly for the convenience of the occupant

- Income received from a limited partnership (a partnership in which you invest money but do not actively participate in the business)

A husband and wife who work together in an Internet sales business can strategize to maximize their eligibility for Social Security benefits. *Chapter 11 discusses this further.*

How to Pay Self-Employment Tax

Self-employment tax is calculated and reported on *IRS Schedule SE (Form 1040): Self-Employment Tax* (**www.irs.gov/pub/irs-pdf/f1040sse.pdf**). You must file *Schedule SE, Schedule C* and *Form 1040* by April 15 after any year in which you have net earnings of $400 or more. If you do not owe any income tax, you must complete *Form 1040* and *Schedule SE* to pay self-employment Social Security tax. This is true even if you already get Social Security benefits.

To pay self-employment tax, you must have a Social Security number (SSN) or an Individual Taxpayer Identification Number (ITIN). *Chapter 3 further discusses such taxes.*

Calculating Your Net Earnings

Your net earnings are essentially your business profit from *Schedule C* minus certain deductions. Under Section 2042 of the Small Business Jobs Act, self-employed individuals can deduct the cost of health insurance in calculating net earnings from self-employment. Wages or salaries from employers who are already withholding Social Security and Medicare tax are not included in your net earnings on *Schedule SE.*

Schedule SE takes you through the process of calculating your self-employment tax on paper. Tax preparation software and some accounting programs will do the calculations for you based on your answers to certain questions.

Optional method

If you had a small profit or a net loss from your business but want to receive credit toward your Social Security coverage, you can use an optional method to compute your net earnings from self-employment. The optional method may increase your earned income credit (EIC) or the child and dependent care credit by increasing your reported income.

The optional method can be used if your gross earnings (your income before you subtract expenses) are $600 or more or when your profit is less than $1,600. You can use the optional method only five times in your life. Your actual net must have been $400 or more in at least two of the last three years, and your net earnings must be less than two-thirds of your gross income.

Here is how it works:

- If your gross income from self-employment is between $600 and $2,400, you may report two-thirds of your gross or your actual net earnings.

- If your gross income is $2,400 (or more) and the actual net earnings are $1,600 (or less), you may report either $1,600 or your actual net earnings.

- Effective tax year 2008 and after, the maximum amount reportable using the optional method of reporting will be equal to the amount needed to get four work credits for a given year. For example, for tax year 2010, the maximum amount reportable using the optional method of reporting would be $4,480 ($1,120 x 4).

Reducing Your Self-Employment Tax

The only way to reduce the amount you pay in self-employment tax is to reduce the net profits from your business (reported on *Schedule C*) by increasing your business expenses. *Chapters 4, 5, and 6 offer suggestions for increasing your business expenses.* Deductions that reduce your personal income tax do not affect your earned income on which self-employment tax is calculated.

There are several reasons why you might not want to reduce your self-employment tax. Although you pay less money in taxes for that year, self-employment taxes pay for benefits you receive in the future. For example, to be eligible for full Social Security benefits you must have at least 40 quarter credits (QCs) by the age of 62 — one quarter credit equals $1,120. Your Social Security payments after you retire are computed based on the amounts you earned yearly during your working life. If you want to receive maximum Social Security benefits in the future, it is best not to under-report your earnings. You can learn more about Social Security eligibility and benefits from the *Annual Statistical Supplement, Social Security (Old-Age, Survivors, and Disability Insurance) Program Description and Legislative History*, published by the SSA Office of Retirement and Disability Policy (**www.ssa.gov/policy/docs/statcomps/supplement/2010/oasdi.html**).

CHAPTER 9

Quarterly Estimated Tax Payments

The United States income tax is a pay-as-you-go tax, which means that tax must be paid as you earn or receive your income during the year. You can either do this through withholding tax from wages or other payments you receive or by making estimated tax payments. If you do not pay your tax through withholding, or do not pay enough tax that way, you might also have to pay estimated taxes. Estimated tax payments are made in four installments, known as quarterly estimated tax payments, throughout the year. First-time online sellers are sometimes unaware that they must make these quarterly tax payments, and they end up faced with unexpected tax bills and penalties. The IRS charges a penalty for underpaying estimated taxes and for late payments. To avoid penalties, determine early in the year whether you are required to make these quarterly payments, and be sure to send in your payments before the deadlines.

Sole proprietors, partners, S corporation shareholders, and self-employed individuals generally have to make estimated tax payments if they expect to owe tax of $1,000 or more when they file their tax returns at the end of the year and if the amount withheld by an employer will equal less than 90 percent of what they owe. You have to make estimated tax payments for your corporation if you expect it to owe tax of $500 or more when you file its annual tax return. You can pay your self-employment taxes as part of quarterly estimated tax payments.

You do not have to pay quarterly estimated taxes if you owed no taxes for the previous 12-month tax year. If you had a tax liability for the previous year, you might have to pay estimated tax for the current year.

Ask your employer to withhold more taxes

If you are working for an employer who is withholding taxes from your paycheck, you can ask to increase the amount withheld to cover taxes on the income from your online sales business. You will not need to pay the quarterly estimated tax if your employer is withholding 90 percent or more of what you will owe at the end of the year. To do this, file a new *Form W-4: Employee's Withholding Allowance Certificate*, with your employer. If you receive a pension or annuity, you can use *Form W-4P, Withholding Certificate for Pension or Annuity Payments*, to start or change your withholding from these payments. You also can choose to have federal income tax withheld from certain government payments. For details, see *Form W-4V, Voluntary Withholding Request*.

The IRS gives you two methods for estimating your tax liability, the "safe harbor" Method and the "SWAG" method. The safe harbor method is used when your income fluctuates from month to month. Look at your tax liability from the previous year, increase that number by 10 percent and divide the result by four to get the amount you must pay each quarter. At the end of the year, any amount you have overpaid in earlier quarters will be deducted from your final payment or refunded to you.

Safe harbor method for calculating quarterly estimated tax payments

Tax liability from previous year	$5,000
PLUS 10%	$5,500
Divided by 4	$1,375
Estimated quarterly tax payment	$1,375

Many people do not expect their income to increase by 10 percent every year and use the SWAG (a U.S. Army acronym for scientific wild-ass guess) method instead. This method requires you to evaluate your accounts and try to estimate how much you owe the IRS for the upcoming quarter. Instead of a fixed quarterly payment, you pay income tax based on how much you earn from one quarter to the next. This method can be risky because if you underpay during the year, then you will owe the remainder in one lump payment to the IRS on April 15, and you may owe penalties. In spite of the risk, most online sellers use this method because there is no real way to determine how much profit you will make from online sales in any one quarter. You might earn much more in one quarter than you did in another. With the safe harbor method, you are likely to overpay in earlier quarters, which means that you are sinking money into taxes that you could have used to buy inventory. Of course, you will get it back at the end of the year, but it is money that could have earned additional profit for your business.

How to Calculate Your Quarterly Estimated Taxes

To determine your estimated quarterly tax payments, you must calculate your expected AGI, taxable income, taxes, deductions, and credits for this year. You can use your previous year's tax return to use as a guide. If your earnings and your circumstances this year will be similar to last year, you can divide last year's tax payment by four. Do not forget to account for specific circumstances that might affect your AGI, such as having fewer dependents living with you this year or having a large itemized medical expense in one year. Changes to government tax laws, such as the 2011 reduction in Social Security tax, might also alter your expected AGI.

IRS Publication 505: Tax Withholding and Estimated Tax (**http://www.irs. gov/pub/irs-pdf/p505.pdf**) contains a worksheet for figuring your estimated quarterly tax payments. Your tax preparation software will walk you through the steps and calculate it for you automatically, and you can use some accounting programs if they contain information from your previous year's tax return. There is also a worksheet for recalculating your quarterly payment if your circumstances change, for example, if your income drops because you withdraw from an online marketplace. Make sure you pay enough each quarter to avoid underpayment penalties. Penalties are calculated separately on each quarterly payment. You could owe a penalty even if you are due a refund at the end of the year.

If you have seasonal income or your income fluctuates substantially during the year, you may owe less tax during some periods. The annualized income installment method annualizes your tax at the end of each period based on a reasonable estimate of your income, deductions, and other items relating to events that occurred from the beginning of the tax year through the end of the period. Use the *Annualized Estimated Tax Worksheet* in *IRS Publication 505* to calculate whether you can pay less estimated tax for some periods. You should use the annualized installment method if you began or ended your business during the year and were not in operation for the full 12 months.

How to Pay Quarterly Estimated Taxes

The due dates for quarterly estimated taxes are typically April 15, June 15, September 15, and January 15, or the next business day if one of these dates falls on a weekend. You can pay the entire amount in advance for the year on April 15 if you wish. The final payment, which is due on January 15 after the end of the tax year, can be ignored if you file your annual tax return and pay the balance in full before January 31.

There are five ways to pay:

- Credit an overpayment of taxes from the previous year. If you have an overpayment when you file your tax return, you can indicate on *Form 1040* that you want to apply it to the next year's quarterly estimated tax. Remember to subtract that amount when calculating your estimated tax payments. If you file by April 15, the overpayment can take care of the payment due.

- Mail a check or money order accompanied by an *Estimated Tax Payment Voucher* from *Form 1040-ES*. You may have received a Form 1040-ES package from the IRS in the mail; if not, then you can order one from the IRS. Use the enclosed window envelopes, and be sure to write your Social Security number on your check. If you and your spouse are filing together, write both of your Social Security numbers. The payment is on time if it is postmarked on or before the due date.

- Pay electronically using the Electronic Federal Tax Payment System (EFTPS).

- Pay by electronic funds withdrawal (EFW) if you are filing *Form 1040* electronically.

- Pay by credit or debit card using a pay-by-phone system or the Internet.

You can find more information about making electronic payments on the IRS website at the Electronic Payment Options Home Page (**www.irs.gov/efile/article/0,,id=97400,00.html**).

Calculating Penalties for Underpayments and Late Payments

You may be penalized if you pay too little estimated tax during any quarter or if a payment is late. The penalty is assessed on the unpaid amount for each day the payment is late or insufficient. The penalty is equal to paying interest at market rates on the amount you underpaid, for the period of the underpayment. The interest rates are adjusted at regular intervals. During most of 2009, 2010, and 2011, the rate was 4 percent. If the underpayment is small and you do not leave it unpaid for a long period, the penalty will be modest.

Use *Form 2210, Underpayment of Estimated Tax by Individuals, Estates, and Trusts*, (**www.irs.gov/pub/irs-pdf/f2210.pdf**) to see if you owe a penalty for underpaying your estimated tax. This calculation is complicated; if you do not want to do it, you can just wait until the IRS calculates it for you and sends you a bill. The only time you might want to calculate it for yourself is when you want to ask for a waiver of part of the penalty. If you received most of your income in the last few months of the year, you can use the annualized income installment method to calculate a lower penalty on *Form 2210*. You should not be penalized for making smaller quarterly estimated payments during the early months of the year when you had little income.

State Income Tax

Many states also require quarterly estimated income tax payments, though the rules and penalties might differ from those from federal income tax. If you live in a state where you pay state income tax, check on the website of your state taxing authority, or call them to see whether you must make estimated tax payments and how to calculate and remit them.

CHAPTER 10

Sales and Use Tax

Sales tax is a surtax imposed on retail sales on the state or local level to collect revenue for schools, police and fire departments, and other services. The sales tax is a percentage of the retail price for which an item is sold. That percentage typically is decided at the local level by a county government or taxing district. Sales tax in the U.S. is complex. Forty-five states charge sales tax; Alaska, Montana, New Hampshire, Oregon, and Delaware do not, although some local districts in Alaska do. Among the states that have a sales tax, there are 7,500 taxing districts, each with its own sales tax rate and rules about what can and cannot be taxed. Local taxing districts often add additional percentages to the state sales tax rate.

Most states' sales tax rates are 6 percent to 8 percent, but some are higher or lower. Most states do not charge sales tax on groceries, prescription drugs, or agricultural supplies. Each state has its own rules about whether certain luxury foods, such as chocolate and candy, should be taxed. In addition, many states legislate annual "sales tax holidays" that suspend the sales tax for a specific period or on specific items to make essential supplies more affordable for low-income families. For example, Florida has a tax holiday for clothing and school supplies for several days before schools open in the fall. Sales tax holidays often are implemented after natural disasters to help local residents with recovery.

Sales tax typically is collected at the cash register when an item is sold, and the retailer is responsible for collecting the tax, filing a return, and remitting the money to the state treasury. Cash registers are programmed to calculate the sales tax automatically, print the amount on receipts, and report sales tax amounts separately from sales.

For online sellers, sales tax is a complicated matter. Should the customer pay you the sales tax rate for your local taxing district, or for the state and district in which he or she lives? Are you supposed to collect sales tax and remit it to each state where you shipped an item? How do you know how much sales tax to charge, and how is that reflected in your shopping cart and payment system?

Federal and State Sales Tax Legislation

A 1992 Supreme Court decision, *Quill Corp. v. North Dakota*, on a case concerning a catalog mail-order company, ruled that retailers are exempt from collecting sales taxes in states where they have no physical presence (nexus), such as a store, office, or warehouse. The Supreme Court commented that requiring mail-order companies to comply with the varied sales tax rules and regulations would burden interstate commerce. That ruling has been applied to online sales businesses ever since. You are required to collect sales tax only on sales of items sold or shipped to someone in the state where your business is located. For a time, large retailers with mortar-and-bricks stores in many locations got around this requirement by setting up their web-based sales as separate business entities so they would not have to charge sales tax. Several states passed legislation making this illegal, and in 2003, several large retailers negotiated with states for amnesty on past uncollected sales tax in return for collecting sales tax in the future.

As Internet commerce has expanded, states have become increasingly concerned about lost revenue from uncollected sales tax on Internet sales. Sales tax revenues are currently about $150 billion annually and make up approximately one-third of all state revenues. A 2009 study by the University of Tennessee estimated the loss at $7.7 billion for 2008. States that charge no personal income tax, such as Texas and Florida, rely primarily on sales tax revenue to fund their government, schools, and public services. As state budgets became increasingly underfunded during the recession, state governments began to look for ways to enforce sales taxes on Internet sales.

Retailers are unable to compete with online sellers whose prices are 4 percent to 9 percent lower because they do not have to charge sales tax. Customers now go into retail stores to examine merchandise and try on clothes and shoes, then go home and buy the products online so they do not have to pay sales tax.

In 2002, the National Governors Association initiated the Streamlined Sales Tax Project (SSUTA) (**www.streamlinedsalestax.org**) to standardize and simplify state tax codes and make collection of sales tax easier. As of June 2011, 44 states and the District of Columbia had approved an interstate agreement that establishes uniform sales tax rules and definitions, and 24 of these states had passed legislation to conform to the agreement. Another nine states are considering similar legislation. States and cities still have the authority to decide tax rates and what goods will be taxed, but must follow rules about matters such as the procedure for changing tax rates, and use a set of uniform definitions (for example, whether marshmallows are considered food or candy for tax purposes).

In the *Quill Corp. v. North Dakota* ruling, the Supreme Court judges said the U.S. Congress "is ... free to decide whether, when, and to what extent the states may burden interstate mail-order concerns with a duty to collect use taxes." So far, Congress has made no ruling on a federal level, but based on the simplified sales tax codes, states and retailers are lobbying Congress to impose federal regulations mandating payment of sales tax on Internet sales. The Main Street Fairness Act (**www.opencongress.org/bill/111-h5660/show**), first introduced in 2009, would require all sellers (except small businesses that qualify for an exemption) to collect sales tax on purchases made by residents of the 24 states that have passed legislation conforming with SSUTA. The act requires the governing board of SSUTA to establish an exemption for small businesses that would not have the resources to keep track of all the state sales tax laws, but the requirements for the exemption have not yet been determined.

The Main Street Fairness Act did not pass in 2009 or 2010, but eventually, you can expect some sort of legislation governing sales tax on online sales. Check regularly with your state sales tax office for updates and the latest rules.

Nexus

Even when a state requires its residents to pay sales tax on digital downloads or merchandise sold online, online retailers are required to collect the sales tax only when they have nexus, a legal term referring to a physical presence, in that state. The criteria for determining whether a business has nexus are different from one state to another. Refer to your state sales tax office for more information.

A business might be considered to have nexus if it has a physical location in the state; it has resident employees working in the state; it has employees, such as sales reps, who regularly solicit business in that state; or it owns property (including intangible property) in that state. In the past, to have nexus for sales tax purposes, a business had to have a physical location in the state, but more recently, some states have expanded this requirement to include affiliates who sell a company's products. The billing address for the credit card used to make the purchase determines the state in which the sale was made and the amount of sales tax to be charged. In sales of merchandise, such as a CD or T-shirt that is physically shipped to a buyer, the shipping address determines the state in which the sale was made and the amount to be charged. Sales tax may be calculated as a percentage of the final price including shipping or as a percentage of the final price of each item sold before shipping is added to the invoice.

EBay and Amazon actively oppose new sales tax legislation

EBay and Amazon know their success is driven by the fact that their prices are often lower than prices in retail stores and not having to pay sales tax keeps those prices low. The economic recession that began in 2007 has pushed even more customers to look for tax-free bargains online. Large retailers, such as Walmart and Sears, and retailer associations have been lobbying state governments to pass legislation enforcing sales tax collection. State governments themselves are facing large budget deficits and looking at sales tax as a way to bring in more revenue. Since 2008, Texas, Colorado, Illinois, Hawaii, North Carolina, Rhode Island, Connecticut, and California have passed laws extending the definition of nexus to include the presence of affiliate sellers — individuals who post links or ads on their websites for an online retailer's products and receive a commission for each sale — in a state. In response, Amazon cut its ties with its affiliates in those states. At least ten other states are threatened with similar cut-offs. Amazon is also disputing the payment of $269 million in sales tax which Texas demanded after determining that Amazon's warehouse in Dallas, owned by a subsidiary, qualified as nexus under state tax rules. Amazon is threatening to close the Texas warehouse and to pull out of planned warehouse projects in South Carolina and Tennessee if it is not exempted from paying sales tax in those states. Amazon pays sales tax in Kansas, Kentucky, New York, North Dakota, and Washington, where it has offices.

EBay opposes any form of legislation that would impose taxes on small retailers, including those who sell goods on its online marketplace.

Large online marketplaces want to avoid having to collect and remit sales tax on behalf of their sellers on the grounds that the process would be too cumbersome. However, retailers, such as Walmart, Best Buy®, and Barnes & Noble, already are collecting and remitting sales tax on their online sales, and Amazon already manages Target's online sales and shipping operations. With the technology available today, it would be possible for online marketplaces to automate the collection and remittance of sales tax for their sellers if they chose to do so.

Use Tax

You only have to collect and pay sales tax for sales made to customers living in states where your company has a physical presence. Customers living in the other states where online sales are taxable are responsible to report and pay sales tax themselves for items they bought online. When the customer pays sales tax directly to his or her state, it is called a use tax. Use tax can be reported and paid online at most state taxing authority websites or submitted using a paper return. Some states, such as New York, include a line on their state income tax returns for use tax on Internet, mail order, and out-of-state purchases. It is difficult for states to enforce a use tax on every online purchase. Many people are unaware that use tax exists. Even if they are aware, the likelihood that they will remember to keep a record of every small online purchase is slim. Because so many purchases are now made online, states such as California are conducting campaigns to educate their residents about use tax.

You may be liable to pay use tax on items that you purchase online from out of state for your personal use or for your business, such as packaging materials, electronics, and computer software, that would have been subject to sales tax if you had bought them at a retail outlet in your state. *Chapter 3 discussed this further.* Items that you buy for resale or raw materials you use to manufacture items for sale are not subject to use tax because they will be subject to sales tax later when they are sold. Keep a separate spreadsheet or ledger page listing the items you buy that are subject to use tax, and make copies of applicable receipts for verification.

Getting a Sales Tax Number

To collect and remit sales tax, you must get a resellers' license or a sales tax certificate from the taxing authority in your state, usually called the State Department of Treasury, State Department of Taxation, or State Department of Revenue. You can find links to each state's taxing authority on the website of the Federation of Tax Administrators (**www.taxadmin.org/fta/link**). Many states allow you to sign up online. Your taxing authority will provide you with an online account or send you paper coupons and envelopes so you can submit a monthly sales tax return and your payment. Be careful to submit your payments on time every month, or you will be charged late penalties. You also can obtain detailed information from the taxing authority about items that are subject to sales tax in your state.

A sales tax certificate serves several purposes. It allows you to obtain wholesale merchandise and raw materials without paying sales tax on them. Most wholesalers will not sell to you unless you give them a copy of your sales tax certificate, and you must show the certificate to gain entry to wholesale trade shows and merchandise marts. Many banks require one to open a commercial bank account.

When you contact your state taxing authority, be sure to get the following details:

- How often do I need to forward sales and use taxes?
- What specific items are or are not taxable?
- What is the tax rate?
- What is the process for forwarding taxes?
- What assistance is available to me by way of forms or advice?

You can find a summary of sales tax requirements by state online at outright.com. (**http://education.outright.com/state-sales-tax-rates-and-requirements-by-state**).

How to Collect Sales Tax

In response to the recent flurry of state legislation concerning sales tax on Internet purchases, several online marketplaces have launched applications that allow sales tax to be added to an item during checkout if it is being shipped to an address in the state(s) where the seller has nexus. You must set up your own account with sales tax preferences. Read the instruction for your online marketplace carefully. The money comes directly to you, and you are responsible to remit it to your state taxing authority.

Sales tax is recorded in your accounts as income, but it becomes an expense when you remit it the state. It passes through your accounting system and does not appear in your final calculations of profit and loss. You should keep a separate ledger or spreadsheet to record sales tax collected for each transaction and the amounts remitted to your state taxing authority. Most bookkeeping software allows you to set up a sales tax account to capture these amounts automatically when you import sales data to your records. Any amount you overcharge for sales tax, either accidentally or because amounts are rounded up to the next cent, belongs to the state. You cannot get extra money from customers by overcharging for sales tax.

Each online marketplace automatically charges and processes sales tax for its sales in states where it has nexus. Here are the procedures for sellers on some of the major online marketplaces:

PayPal

If you collect payment for auctions through PayPal, you can program it to collect sales tax automatically from customers in your state. However, PayPal takes its commission based on the total amount of the sale, so you will be paying commission on the sales tax as well as the retail price of the item. To compensate for this, you can add a few cents to the shipping and handling fee for your item when you list it.

EBay

You can use the eBay tax table to specify a sales tax rate for each U.S. state in which you are required to charge sales tax. There is also an option for charging sales tax on shipping and handling, if that is required by your state. Your sales tax rates will show on your item page, and the correct sales tax is calculated and added to the total price during checkout. You are responsible for reporting the sales tax and remitting it to your state taxing authority.

Amazon Marketplace

Currently Amazon Marketplace leaves the collection of sales tax completely up to the seller. According to Amazon.com, "Marketplace sellers are responsible for the sales tax on any items sold on Amazon.com, and if necessary, they generally add this cost into the price of their items." This means you either have to raise the price of your item for all buyers to include the sales tax, or risk taking a loss if someone in your state happens to buy your item.

Information about Amazon's sales tax policy for its own sales can be found on its website under Sales Tax Requirements (**www.amazon.com/gp/help/ customer/display.html?nodeId=468512**). If an item is subject to sales tax in the state to which the order is shipped, tax generally is calculated on the total selling price of each individual item, which typically includes "item-level shipping and handling charges, item-level discounts, gift-wrap charges, and an allocation of order-level shipping and handling charges and order-level discounts."

For electronically downloaded products, such as e-books, music videos, and MP3 files, the ZIP code of the billing address for the credit card used to pay for the purchase determines whether sales tax is charged. If you are selling a book or music that you published through CreateSpace™ (**www.createspace.com**), Amazon's on-demand publishing arm, Amazon will collect and process the sales tax. Amazon also processes sales tax for some of its large retailers, including Target, Dow Jones, Penguin Books, and *The New York Times.*

Bonanza

In May 2011, Bonanza launched a test of a new in-house application that lets sellers select the states and ZIP codes for which they need to apply sales tax to their orders. The sales tax is applied after the shipping destination has been entered in the shopping cart, after any discounts have been applied, and is included in the total amount for the order. Sellers can choose whether the sales tax is applied to shipping and handling. Sellers also can create special offers that include sales tax and shipping in the price of the item, so the customer pays only the advertised price. Sales tax information is not reported to taxing authorities, and it is up to the sellers to remit sales taxes to their state taxing authorities.

Etsy.com

Sellers on etsy.com can enter rates for each state, province, or ZIP code for which they want to charge sales tax. Sales tax is automatically added to the order during the checkout process. It is up to sellers to remit sales taxes to their state taxing authorities.

Though you technically should collect sales tax on any item sold to a customer in your state, most taxing authorities are probably not concerned about casual sellers selling a few inexpensive items every year. They will be taking a closer look at businesses that carry on a heavy Internet trade or sell big-ticket items. Learn about your online marketplace's sales tax policies, and develop your own strategy for complying with your state's sales tax laws. This is a time of change in the e-commerce arena, and online marketplaces are changing and adding features and policies all the time. Keep your eyes open for new developments that might affect your business.

Sales Tax Service Providers

Sales tax rates and regulations are changing continually. It would be impossible for a small business, or even a large online retailer, to keep up with all the new laws being passed in 7,500 taxing districts. Instead, large retailers use third-party tax service providers, companies dedicated to researching and cataloging sales tax rates. These companies provide continually updated databases of sales tax rates by ZIP code and taxing district. Online shopping carts and accounting software programs draw on this data to calculate sales tax on individual purchases. Accounting software programs, such as QuickBooks, include sales-tax modules that calculate how much sales tax should be charged for each sale based on your physical location and the shipping or billing address of your customer, and they keep track of the amount you owe each month. Some third-party providers also collect the sales taxes and remit them to each state on behalf of the retailers.

Third-party sales tax providers include Avalara (**www.avalara.com**), Automatic Data Processing Inc. (ADP®) (**www.adp.com**), Exactor (**www. exactor.com**), SpeedTax™ (**www.speedtax.com**), and TaxTools™ (**www. accuratetax.com**). Large online marketplaces make their services available to you through their sales tax applications. The correct sales tax is calculated for each sale based on the billing or shipping address, and your account shows how much sales tax you have collected each month.

If you sell through your own online shopping cart instead of selling through an online marketplace and need to add sales tax capability, FedTax – Tax-Cloud (**http://taxcloud.net**) is a free service that allows online merchants to calculate and remit destination-based sales tax.

CHAPTER 11

Working with a Spouse or Family Member

Many online sales businesses are family operations, with married couples working together to locate items for sale and prepare them for shipping. You might have your parent or child helping you with some aspect of your business. Because family members working together share more than just their work space, the IRS treats them slightly differently from individual sole proprietors. The way you file your taxes could have long-term consequences on your Social Security benefits, as well as on how much you save for retirement. Your family members also may make you eligible for certain tax breaks on your personal income tax return.

The IRS treats a husband-and-wife team operating a small business such as an online sales business differently for tax purposes than an ordinary business partnership.

Qualified Joint Venture

The Small Business and Work Opportunity Tax Act of 2007, signed into law May 25, 2007, allows a husband-and-wife business to be treated as a "qualified joint venture" instead of a partnership for federal tax purposes. This allows both husband and wife to report income from the business without having to file *Form 1065, U.S. Return of Partnership Income* and *Schedule E: Supplemental Income and Loss* with *Form 1040*. This will save considerable time and money in accounting fees (an accountant typically charges about $1,000 to complete a *Form 1065*). A spouse who does not report earned income does not get the benefit of paying into Social Security, a circumstance that could hurt him or her in the future.

Definition of marriage

For federal tax purposes, a marriage means only a legal union between a man and a woman as husband and wife. *IRS Publication 501(2010): Exemptions, Standard Deduction, and Filing Information* (**www.irs.gov/publications/p501/ar02.html#en_US_2010_publink1000220722**)

Instead, a husband and wife each fill out a separate *Schedule C: Profit or Loss from Business*, and both *Schedule Cs* are attached to their joint tax return. All items of income, gain, loss, deduction, and credit are divided between the spouses according to their respective interests in the business. Each spouse lists his or her respective share of these items on *Schedule C* as a sole proprietor. Husband and wife can divide business incomes, losses, credits, and deductions 50/50 according to how much money each has invested in the business, according to the percentage of the work that each one does, or according to some other mutually acceptable formula. Filing two *Schedule Cs* does not increase or decrease your tax ability, but it gives each of you credit for Social Security benefits. Because each spouse is treated as a sole proprietor, there is no need for either to have an Employer Identification Number (EIN). Each also spouse should fill out a separate *Schedule SE (Form 1040), Self-Employment Tax*, if he or she is paying self-employment taxes.

Income limitation for Social Security earnings

For 2011, the maximum taxable earnings amount for Social Security is $106,800. That means that any amount you earn over that will not increase the amount you can put into Social Security.

The IRS defines a "qualified joint venture" as a joint venture involving the conduct of a trade or business, in which:

(1) The only members of the joint venture are a husband and wife.

(2) Both spouses materially participate in the trade or business.

(3) Both spouses elect to have the provision apply.

(4) The business is co-owned by both spouses and is not held in the name of a state law entity such as a partnership or limited liability company (LLC).

The provision applies only to an active business in which both spouses participate, not to a passive activity, such as joint ownership of rental property.

The "material participation" requirement is met only if each spouse meets one of the following tests:

1. The taxpayer works 500 hours or more during the year in the activity.

2. The taxpayer does substantially all the work in the activity.

3. The taxpayer works more than 100 hours in the activity during the year, and no one else works more than the taxpayer.

4. The taxpayer works more than 100 hours, but fewer than 500, in two or more businesses, and the sum of all the hours in these businesses is more than 500.

5. The taxpayer materially participated in the activity in any 5 of the previous 10 years.

6. The activity is a personal service activity, and the taxpayer materially participated in that activity in any 3 previous years.

7. The taxpayer participates in the activity on a regular, continuous, and substantial basis during such year, working at least 100 hours in the activity, with no one else working more hours than the taxpayer in the activity, and no one else receiving compensation for managing the activity.

A husband-and-wife team can "elect" to file as a qualified joint venture by filing out the *Schedule Cs* and attaching them to their joint tax return. If at some future point they want to alter their status, they must obtain the permission of the IRS. However, the qualified joint venture election ceases automatically in any year the spouses fail to meet the requirements for filing the election.

How to handle requests from the IRS for a partnership return from the spouses for tax years for which the election is in effect

If after filing as qualified joint venture, you receive a notice from the IRS asking for a *Form 1065* for a year in which you and your spouse met the requirements of a qualified joint venture, contact the toll-free number on the notice, and advise the telephone assister that you reported your income on your jointly filed individual income tax return as a qualified joint venture, or send a letter to the address on the notice.

Employer/Employee Relationship

A spouse is considered an employee if there is an employer/employee type of relationship between husband and wife — in other words, if the first spouse substantially controls the business and makes management decisions, and the second spouse is under the direction and control of the first spouse. If your spouse is your employee, not your partner, you must pay Social Security and Medicare taxes for him or her. The wages for the services of an individual who works for his or her spouse in a trade or business are subject to income tax withholding and Social Security and Medicare taxes, but not to FUTA (unemployment) tax. For more information, refer to *IRS Publication 15, Circular E, Employer's Tax Guide* (**www.irs.gov/pub/irs-pdf/p15.pdf**). You will need an EIN in order to pay wages and withhold taxes. *Chapter 1 explains how to obtain an EIN.* The business's half of Social Security and Medicare taxes are deductible as a business expense.

If you and your spouse are a qualified joint venture and hire employees, either of you can report and pay the employment taxes on the wages paid to the employees using the EIN of your sole proprietorship.

If your business is structured as a corporation, putting your spouse on the payroll as an employee is a way of taking some income out of the company and reducing the business tax paid by the corporation. Money you take out of a corporation as a dividend is taxed twice: business tax on the original earnings, and personal income tax on the dividends you receive. Wages paid to your spouse are a business expense and only are taxed once, as part of your spouse's income. Be careful not to make the wages excessive because abnormally high wages are a red flag to the IRS.

Family Members as Employees

Special tax rules apply when you pay a child or a parent to do work for your online sales business. Payments to a child younger than 18 who works for his or her parent in a trade or business are not subject to Social Security and Medicare taxes if the trade or business is a sole proprietorship, qualified joint venture, or a partnership in which each partner is a parent of the child. If these payments are for work other than in a trade or business, such as domestic work in the parent's private home, they are not subject to Social Security and Medicare taxes until the child reaches age 21. Payments for the services of a child younger than 21 who works for his or her parent, whether or not in a trade or business, are not subject to federal unemployment (FUTA) tax.

Payments for the services of a child of any age who works for his or her parent are generally subject to income tax withholding unless the payments are for domestic work in the parent's home. You do not have to withhold income if you pay the child less than $50 per quarter for work other than in a trade or business, or the child is not regularly employed to do such work.

The wages for the services of a child (or spouse) are subject to income tax withholding as well as Social Security, Medicare, and FUTA taxes if he or she works for:

- A corporation, even if it is controlled by the child's parent or the individual's spouse
- A partnership, even if the child's parent is a partner, unless each partner is a parent of the child
- A partnership, even if the individual's spouse is a partner
- An estate, even if it is the estate of a deceased parent

Payments to a parent working in your business are subject to income tax withholding and Social Security and Medicare taxes. Payments for work that is not related to your business are not. Payments made to a parent employed in your business are not subject to FUTA tax.

Family Tax Breaks

Several tax breaks or tax advantages are associated with husband-and-wife businesses and reporting of two incomes instead of one.

Child and Dependent Care credit

If both you and your spouse are active in your Internet sales business, and you have a dependent child age 12 or younger or a dependent of any age who is physically or mentally unable to care for himself or herself, you might qualify for a federal tax credit of up to 35 percent of the cost of day care. In order to claim the credit, you must have earned income, and the day care provided must enable you to work or to look for work. The dependent must live with you and meet the IRS definition of a dependent.

IRS Definition of a Dependent

IRS Publication 501(2010): Exemptions, Standard Deduction, and Filing Information (**www.irs.gov/publications/p501/ar02.html#en_US_2010_publink 1000220722**)

- You cannot claim any dependents if you, or your spouse if filing jointly, could be claimed as a dependent by another taxpayer.

- You cannot claim a married person who files a joint return as a dependent unless that joint return is only a claim for refund and there would be no tax liability for either spouse on separate returns.

- You cannot claim a person as a dependent unless that person is a U.S. citizen, U.S. resident alien, U.S. national, or a resident of Canada or Mexico.[1]

- You cannot claim a person as a dependent unless that person is your **qualifying child** or **qualifying relative**.

Tests To Be a Qualifying Child

1. The child must be your son, daughter, stepchild, foster child, brother, sister, half brother, half sister, stepbrother, stepsister, or a descendant of any of them.

2. The child must be (a) under age 19 at the end of the year and younger than you (or your spouse, if filing jointly), (b) under age 24 at the end of the year, a full-time student, and younger than you (or your spouse, if filing jointly), or (c) any age if permanently and totally disabled.

3. The child must have lived with you for more than half of the year.[2]

4. The child must not have provided more than half of his or her own support for the year.

5. The child is not filing a joint return for the year (unless that joint return is filed only as a claim for refund).

If the child meets the rules to be a qualifying child of more than one person, only one person can actually treat the child as a qualifying child. See the *Special Rule for Qualifying Child of More Than One Person* described later to find out which person is the person entitled to claim the child as a qualifying child.

Tests To Be a Qualifying Relative

1. The person cannot be your qualifying child or the qualifying child of any other taxpayer.

2. The person either (a) must be related to you in one of the ways listed under relatives who do not have to live with you, or (b) must live with you all year as a member of your household[2] (and your relationship must not violate local law).

3. The person's gross income for the year must be less than $3,650.[3]

4. You must provide more than half of the person's total support for the year.[4]

[1]There is an exception for certain adopted children.

[2]There are exceptions for temporary absences, children who were born or died during the year, children of divorced or separated parents or parents who live apart, and kidnapped children.

[3]There is an exception if the person is disabled and has income from a sheltered workshop.

[4]There are exceptions for multiple support agreements, children of divorced or separated parents or parents who live apart, and kidnapped children.

The person who provides child care or adult day-care services cannot be one of your dependents. A day-care provider who is your son or daughter must not be your dependent and must be age 19 or older by the end of the year. The day-care provider must provide you with his or her name, business name (if applicable), address, and either Social Security or Employer Identification Number. This information must be reported on *Form 2441: Child and Dependent Care Expenses* (**www.irs.gov/pub/irs-pdf/f2441. pdf**). The tax credit ranges from 20 percent to 35 percent of your day-care expenses, depending on your AGI. More information can be found in *IRS Publication 503: Child and Dependent Care Expenses* (**www.irs.gov/pub/ irs-pdf/p503.pdf**).

Maximizing Social Security benefits

Dividing business income between husband and wife in a qualified joint venture means that both get credit for paying Social Security taxes. When calculating what percentage of the business income to allocate to each spouse in a husband-and-wife business, consider your future Social Security benefits. Each of you pays Social Security taxes based on the amount of income you report. After retirement age, while both spouses are alive, the spouse that earned less receives whichever is higher: the Social Security benefit based on his or her own earnings, or half of the higher wage earner's benefit. It might be to your advantage to report most of the business income under one spouse so his or her earnings will be higher. When one spouse dies, the survivor receives 100 percent of the deceased spouse's benefits if they are higher than his or her own benefits. By attributing higher earnings to one spouse, both spouses will benefit from his or her higher Social Security payment. Many factors affect your Social Security benefits, including how much Social Security tax you paid at your previous jobs, how long you worked, how much income you are making from your online sales business, whether one of you is disabled, and the age at which you begin taking benefits.

Most people need 10 years of work (40 credits) to qualify for benefits. Your benefit amount is based on your earnings averaged over most of your working career. Higher lifetime earnings result in higher benefits. Your benefits are reduced by a certain percentage if you begin taking them before you reach full retirement age, and if you work while receiving Social Security. As a married couple, you can maximize your Social Security benefits by carefully planning when each of you will sign up to begin receiving payments. For example, if the higher wage earner begins receiving payments before full retirement age, that could reduce the benefit the other spouse will receive. Your health and your life expectancy are another important consideration.

You can get more information about your Social Security benefits from the Benefits Planner on the Social Security Administration's (SSA) website (**www.ssa.gov/planners**), and from advocacy groups, such as the AARP® (**www.aarp.org/work/social-security**). A professional financial planner can help you prepare a strategy for maximizing your retirement income. Most financial planners offer fee-based consultations and financial plans. You can locate a certified financial planner in your area through the National Association of Personal Financial Advisors (NAPFA) (**www.napfa.org**), Financial Planning Association (FPA®) (**www.fpanet.org**), the American Institute of Certified Public Accountants (AICPA®) (**www.aicpa.org**), or your local Better Business Bureau® (**www.bbb.org**).

Travel, entertainment, and education business expenses

When you and your spouse file taxes as a qualified joint enterprise, you can deduct business-related expenses for both of you from your business income. For example, if you travel around to find items for your inventory, attend a trade show or meet with a supplier over dinner during a trip, you can deduct the cost of meals, admission tickets, and other related expenses for both of you. Your combined business expenses will be divided between you on your Schedule Cs, depending on the portion of the business you allocate to each spouse.

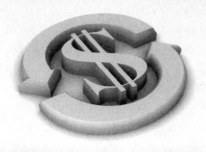

CHAPTER 12

Long-Term Tax Breaks: IRAs, Roth IRAs, and SEPs

M uch of the information in this book helps you keep more of the money you earn from your Internet sales by reducing your taxable income at the end of each tax year. You also should know about the other important tax breaks the IRS gives you over the course of your working life: tax-advantaged retirement savings accounts. Earnings from ordinary investment accounts are taxed each year as either income (dividends, interest income) or capital gains (profit from the sale of stocks, property, and other assets). Because the U.S. government wants to ensure you can save enough for your retirement, however, the IRS allows you to put a certain amount each year into a tax-ad-

vantaged investment account so your savings can grow faster. You can add to the extra income from your Internet sales business by putting it in an IRA and investing it wisely.

There are two basic types of tax-advantaged accounts: traditional IRAs (Individual Retirement Arrangements) and Roth IRAs. A traditional IRA defers income tax on your money until you have retired and are ready to start withdrawing it, essentially giving you another 15 percent to 28 percent of your money to invest. You pay income tax on the money going into a Roth IRA but no taxes at all on the money you withdraw from it. Many taxpayers reduce their taxable income each year by making a last-minute contribution to a traditional IRA, but the tax-free earnings in a Roth IRA, reinvested over time, confer a greater advantage when it is time to take the money out.

The rules governing when and how you put money into an IRA, what you do with it, and when and how you take it out, are strictly enforced by the IRS. The financial penalties imposed when these rules are broken are guaranteed to wipe out any of the benefit you might have derived from the tax-deferred status of an IRA. IRAs were created primarily to help lower-wage earners save money for retirement, so the benefits are phased out gradually for taxpayers with higher incomes. They are regulated closely to prevent abuse, and the IRS imposes penalties for breaking rules and for failing to make withdrawals on time after you retire. Also, you are not allowed to touch the money in an IRA until you reach retirement age, except for a few exemptions, such as $10,000 to make a down payment on a first home. To get the maximum benefit from an IRA, you need to understand the rules and have a basic knowledge of investment principles. Rules for IRAs are found in *IRS Publication 590: Individual Retirement Arrangements (IRAs)* (**www.irs.gov/pub/irs-pdf/p590.pdf**).

Contribution Limits

There is a limit to how much you can contribute to an IRA in one year. The IRS determines this limit, and it is intended to prevent IRAs from being used as tax shelters to amass personal wealth.

- Only an individual with earned income, or one whose spouse has earned income, can contribute to an IRA.

- An individual can contribute up to $5,000 to an IRA for 2011. If you have more than one IRA account, the contribution limit applies to the total amount contributed to all the accounts combined, not to each individual IRA.

- Individuals 50 years of age or older before the end of 2011 can contribute up to $6,000.

- Combined annual contributions to all your IRAs cannot exceed your annual earned income. If your earned income is less than $5,000, then you can contribute only an amount equal to your income for that year.

- You cannot contribute any more to a traditional IRA after you reach the age of 70 ½, even if you are still earning income.

- An IRA is an individual account; the contribution limit for IRAs does not apply to contributions you make to a qualified retirement plan, such as a 401(k), through your employer. If you have a retirement plan at work, all or part of your contribution to your IRA may not be tax-deductible.

- Spouses cannot share an IRA. Each spouse is entitled to open an individual IRA and to contribute up to the maximum annual limit, even if only one spouse has earned income. In 2011, a married couple was allowed to contribute a total of $10,000 to their IRAs (as much as $12,000 if both were 50 or older). The total contribution cannot exceed the couple's combined income.

Contribution Deadlines

Contributions to an IRA can be made at any time before April 15 of the following year, when income tax returns are due. Once the deadline has passed, you cannot contribute any more for that year. If you make a contribution between January 1 and April 15 for the previous year, you must tell the IRA sponsor which year it is intended for; otherwise it will be treated by the IRS as a contribution for the current year. You can claim a deduction on your tax return for an IRA contribution that has not yet been made, as long as you make that contribution before April 15.

Deduct your income tax refund from your taxable income for the same year

You can have your income tax refund, or a portion of it, deposited directly into your IRA as part of your annual contribution. To have your refund deposited directly into your IRA, indicate this on the appropriate line of IRS Form 1040. *IRS Form 8888: Allocation of Refund* (**www.irs.gov/pub/irs-pdf/f8888.pdf**) allows you to divide your refund among up to three different accounts. (Check Box 3, "Savings" for the IRA account.) If you do your taxes a few weeks early and deposit the refund directly into your traditional IRA, you can include it as part of the previous year's IRA contribution and claim it as an income tax deduction. There are no extensions. If the deposit is not made by that date, it will count as an IRA contribution for the next year.

Early distributions — 59 ½ rule

You cannot start taking money out of your IRA before you reach the age of 59 ½. If you are younger than 59 ½ in the year you take a distribution from your traditional IRA, you will be charged a 10-percent tax penalty in addition to ordinary income tax on the amount. The 10-percent penalty on early withdrawals from an IRA is calculated and reported on *IRS Form 5329.* The penalty is intended to discourage workers from using their IRAs as savings accounts or withdrawing funds irresponsibly.

The 10-percent penalty ensures a substantial loss

The 10-percent penalty imposed on early withdrawals from an IRA mirrors the penalty banks charge for the early withdrawal of CDs or closure of savings accounts. Unless the investments in your IRA have been performing unusually well for a long period, the 10-percent penalty effectively guarantees you will lose all earnings and interest on your contribution and probably some of your principal, as well.

Exceptions to the 59 ½ rule

The 10-percent penalty for early withdrawal is waived in several circumstances. Amounts used for these purposes should be reported on line 2 of *IRS Form 5329.* The special circumstances are:

- You have unreimbursed medical expenses that are more than 7.5 percent of your AGI.

- You are unemployed and paid for medical insurance for yourself, your spouse, and your dependents.

- You are disabled.

- You are the beneficiary of a deceased IRA owner.

- You retired early and are receiving distributions as part of a series of equal annual payments (SEPP).

- You paid for qualified higher education expenses during the year of the withdrawal.

- You used up to $10,000 from your IRA to buy, build, or rebuild a first home for yourself or an immediate family member. You can withdraw up to $10,000 from your IRA free of the 10-percent penalty to pay for the costs of buying, building, or rebuilding a home, and any usual or reasonable settlement, financing, or other closing costs. The home can be for you; your spouse; or the parents, other ancestors, children, or grandchildren of you or your spouse. The funds must be used to pay qualified acquisition costs before the close of the 120th day after the day you received the distribution.

The total amount of your qualified first-time home distributions from your IRA cannot exceed $10,000. If both you and your spouse are first-time home buyers, you are each entitled to withdraw up to $10,000 from your IRAs.

- The distribution is due to an IRS levy of the qualified plan to collect unpaid taxes.

- You were a qualified reservist.

- You transferred funds out of your IRA as part of a divorce settlement.

- You withdrew excess contributions to your IRA before the tax deadline.

- You rolled a distribution from your IRA over to another IRA.

Traditional IRA

Depending on how much you earn, all or part of your contribution to a traditional IRA may be deducted from your taxable income for that year. That means you could deduct up to $5,000 from your taxable income or

$6,000 if you are 50 or older. You and your spouse could deduct as much as $12,000 if you are both older than 50.

The amount of the deduction is also affected if you have a retirement savings plan at work through an employer. The amount of the deduction is calculated when you prepare your taxes; tax preparation software does it for you automatically.

Deduction if you do not have a retirement plan at work

FILING STATUS	MODIFIED AGI	DEDUCTION
Single, head of household, or qualifying widow(er)	Any amount	A full deduction up to the amount of your contribution limit
Married filing jointly or **separately** with a spouse who **is not** covered by a plan at work	Any amount	A full deduction up to the amount of your contribution limit
Married filing jointly with a spouse who **is** covered by a plan at work	$169,000 or less	A full deduction up to the amount of your contribution limit
	More than $169,000 but less than $179,000	A partial deduction
	$179,000 or more	No deduction
Married filing separately with a spouse who is covered by a plan at work	Less than $10,000	A partial deduction
	$10,000 or more	No deduction
If you file separately and did not live with your spouse at any time during the year, your IRA deduction is determined under the "single" filing status.		

Deduction if you have a retirement plan at work

FILING STATUS	MODIFIED AGI	DEDUCTION
Single or head of household	$56,000 or less	A full deduction up to the amount of your contribution limit
	More than $56,000 but less than $66,000	A partial deduction
	$66,000 or more	No deduction

FILING STATUS	MODIFIED AGI	DEDUCTION
Married filing jointly or **qualifying widow**	$90,000 or less	A full deduction up to the amount of your contribution limit
	More than $90,000 but less than $110,000	A partial deduction
	$110,000 or more	No deduction
Married filing separately	Less than $10,000	A partial deduction
	$10,000 or more	No deduction
If you file separately and did not live with your spouse at any time during the year, your IRA deduction is determined under the "single" filing status.		

You do not pay income tax on the money you put into your traditional IRA, but you do pay income tax on all the money you withdraw from it. The year you turn 70 ½, you must begin drawing a specific amount, your Required Minimum Withdrawal (RMD), whether you need the money or not, and paying income tax on it. The RMD is calculated to ensure that your retirement savings are steadily depleted during your retirement and that the IRS gets its taxes. If you miss the deadline for a withdrawal, or fail to withdraw enough money, you will incur penalties.

The amounts not deducted from your taxable income are called nondeductible contributions and are not taxed because you already paid tax on them in the year they were contributed. A nondeductible contribution is the total amount of your contribution for that year minus the amount you are allowed as a tax deduction. The nondeductible contributions you make to an IRA are known as your "basis."

Excess contributions to an IRA are assessed a 6-percent excise tax that cancels out any investment gains you might make from them.

Roth IRA

Roth IRAs were created by the *Taxpayer Relief Act of 1997 (Public Law 105-34)*, and named for the bill's sponsor, Senator William Roth of Delaware. Roth IRAs are intended to convey additional investment benefits to low-income earners and are structured differently from traditional IRAs. You do not get an instant tax deduction for contributions to a Roth IRA because they are made after income tax has been paid on them. Unlike the earnings in a traditional IRA, which are taxed as regular income when they are distributed, the earnings in a Roth IRA are tax-free income. They are never taxed as long as the account has been in existence for more than five years and the owner is older than 59 ½ years old when they are withdrawn, the withdrawal is made because of the death or disability of the owner, or $10,000 is withdrawn for the purchase of a first home.

If you qualify to have one, a Roth IRA has several advantages. No matter how wildly successful your investments are, you will never pay taxes on any of those earnings or profits. The money you contribute to your Roth IRA is still available to you if you need it for an emergency; in the meantime, it is earning investment income.

- Unlike with traditional IRAs, you can continue contributing to a Roth IRA after you reach age 70 ½ as long as you or your spouse continues to have earned income. You cannot contribute more than your earned income for the year.

- You cannot contribute anything to a Roth IRA if your modified Adjusted Gross Income (AGI) exceeds a certain limit. The chart below shows the income limits for 2011. Those in the lowest income brackets can make the full contribution each year; reduced contributions are allowed for those in intermediate income brackets. Detailed instructions for figuring your modified AGI and calculating your contribution limit for a Roth IRA can be found in *IRS Publication 590, Roth IRAs* (**http://www.irs.gov/publications/ p590/ch02.html#en_US_publink10006503**).

Contribution limits for Roth IRAs

FILING STATUS	MODIFIED AGI	
Married filing jointly or **qualifying widow(er)**	Less than $169,000	You can contribute up to the limit.
	At least $169,000 but less than $179,000	The amount you can contribute is reduced.
	$179,000 or more	You cannot contribute to a Roth IRA.
Married filing separately and you lived with your spouse at any time during the year	Zero (-0-)	You can contribute up to the limit.
	More than zero (-0-) but less than $10,000	The amount you can contribute is reduced.
	$10,000 or more	You cannot contribute to a Roth IRA.
Single, head of household, or **married filing separately** and you did not live with your spouse at any time during the year	Less than $107,000	You can contribute up to the limit.
	At least $107,000 but less than $122,000	The amount you can contribute is reduced.
	$122,000 or more	You cannot contribute to a Roth IRA.

- **Contributions can be withdrawn any time without penalty.**
  A Roth IRA consists of two portions: the contributions you make
  to the account and the earnings from the stocks, bonds, funds,
  and other investments held in the account. Because income tax has
  already been paid on the contributions to a Roth IRA, they can be
  withdrawn at any time without a penalty, even a few days after they
  were made.

Earnings are not withdrawn from a Roth IRA until after all of the contributions have been distributed. The 59 ½ rule still applies to the earnings in a Roth IRA, but the IRA owner will not be taxed if they are qualified distributions. A worksheet for calculating the taxable portion of a distribution from a Roth IRA can be found in *IRS Publication 590, Roth IRAs,*

"How Do You Figure the Taxable Part?" (**www.irs.gov/publications/p590/ch02.html#en_US_2010_publink1000231076**).

- **Qualified distributions are not taxed.** The earnings from investments in your Roth IRA will not be taxed as long as they are qualified distributions. To take a qualified distribution, you must have held the Roth IRA for at least five years and have one of the qualifying characteristics: older than 59 ½, disabled, or withdrawing up to $10,000 for the purchase of a first home. The five-year period begins on January 1 of the first year for which you contribute. If you contribute for the previous year just before the tax-filing deadline on April 15, that previous year counts as the first year.

- **The earnings part of nonqualified distributions may be subject to taxation.** A nonqualified distribution is a withdrawal from a Roth IRA made before you reach age 59 ½ or before the completion of the five-year holding period that begins on January 1 of the year that you make your first contribution. Your contributions are never taxed when you take a distribution from the account, but any earnings that are part of a nonqualified withdrawal are taxed as regular income. A worksheet for calculating the taxable portion of a distribution from a Roth IRA can be found in *IRS Publication 590, Roth IRAs, "How Do You Figure the Taxable Part?"* (**www.irs.gov/publications/p590/ch02.html#en_US_2010_publink1000231076**).

- **No required minimum distribution.** There is no RMD for Roth IRAs. Income tax already has been paid on contributions to a Roth IRA, and earnings can be withdrawn tax-free once all requirements are met. The IRS has no incentive to force withdrawals from a Roth IRA so that it can collect deferred taxes, as it does with traditional IRAs. The owner can leave the funds in a Roth IRA untouched, continuing to increase in value until his or her death, when it passes to a beneficiary or an heir.

Converting to a Roth IRA

Even if you earn too much income to contribute to a Roth IRA, you are allowed to convert your traditional IRA or 401(k) to a Roth, pay all the income tax due, and withdraw all future earnings tax free. If you have a profitable year and can afford to pay the income tax with funds outside the IRA, converting to a Roth guarantees you tax-free income in the future.

An IRA cannot be liquidated during a bankruptcy

Assets held in a retirement fund, including a self-directed IRA, are protected from creditors. The Employee Retirement Income Security Act of 1974 (ERISA) is a federal law that sets minimum standards for retirement and health benefit plans in private industry. ERISA protects assets held in qualified retirement plans from legal process, as long as the plan document has the proper "anti-alienation" clauses. (Anti-alienation clauses do not allow ownership of assets to be transferred to a third-party, i.e. a creditor). ERISA keeps these plans from being liquidated during a bankruptcy. The U.S. Supreme Court concluded in *Rousey v. Jacoway* (April 2005), that IRAs were "exempt from the reach of their creditors." Bankruptcy laws have been amended to exempt all IRAs from collectors if the IRA holder goes bankrupt.

Beneficiaries

An IRA is not bequeathed to your heirs in your will. It goes directly to the beneficiaries listed on the IRA beneficiary form. If an IRA owner dies before reaching age 70 ½, the entire IRA typically must be distributed by the end of the fifth year after the year of the owner's death or paid out as RMDs based on the life expectancy of the beneficiary. These RMDs must begin in the calendar year following the year in which the IRA owner died. The beneficiary pays income tax on distributions from a traditional IRA, but distributions from a Roth IRA are tax-free income. A spouse who is a sole beneficiary of an IRA can delay the RMDs until the year after the IRA owner would have reached age 70 ½. A spouse also has the option of taking ownership of the IRA and treating it as if it were his or her own.

Simplified Employee Pension (SEP) IRAs

Under a Simplified Employee Pension (SEP) plan, an employer contributes to traditional Individual Retirement Arrangements (IRAs) set up for employees. A business of any size, including a self-employed individual, can set up a SEP as long as the business does not have any other pension plan. A SEP is funded only by employer contributions; employees cannot make contributions of their own. Each employee has complete ownership (is 100 percent vested) in his or her SEP-IRA.

To set up a SEP, find a financial institution to act as your trustee. The trustee will receive and invest contributions and provide an annual statement and explanation of any fees and commissions. Some trustees offer services, such as statements and the ability to reallocate investments online. Next, create a written agreement including your name, the requirements for employee participation, the signature of a responsible official, and a definite formula for allocating contributions. The formula for deciding annual contributions can be based on the earnings of the business for each year. The IRS offers a model agreement, *Form 5305-SE, Simplified Employee Pension — Individual Retirement Accounts Contribution Agreement*. Most financial institutions have a prototype document, or you can draw up an agreement of your own. The SEP is not considered adopted until all eligible employees have received documents and information required by the IRS.

Set up a traditional IRA for each eligible employee with the trustee(s). A SEP plan may be established and the first contributions made as late as the due date (including extensions) of your business income tax return for the year.

A SEP-IRA is a traditional IRA and is subject to the same rules and re-strictions regarding minimum required distributions, early withdrawals, and beneficiaries.

Total contributions to each employee's IRA cannot exceed $49,000 for 2011 or 25 percent of the employee's pay. Business owners or self-employed individuals who take a net profit from their business rather than a salary can contribute up to 20 percent of their net profit for the year, subject to contribution limits. Sole proprietors and partners may deduct contributions for themselves on *Form 1040, U.S. Individual Income Tax Return.* (If you are a partner, contributions for yourself are shown on the *Schedule K-1 (Form 1065), Partner's Share of Income, Credits, Deductions, etc.).* Contributions to a SEP-IRA will not affect the amount an individual employee can contribute to a Roth IRA because the contributions to the SEP are made by the employer rather than by the individual.

A SEP can be terminated by notifying the trustee that it will no longer be making contributions to the employee IRAs. The business does not have to notify the IRS when it terminates a SEP.

Advantages of a SEP

The employer can deduct contributions to a SEP from taxable profit, and employees do not include contributions to a SEP-IRA in their gross income for the year. SEP contributions are not subject to federal income tax withholding, Social Security, Medicare, and Federal Unemployment Taxes (FUTA). Self-employment income often fluctuates from year to year. A SEP can be set up to allow contributions equal to a fixed portion of the annual income from a business, so in good years, a larger amount can be excluded from taxable profit.

The contribution limits for SEP-IRAs are much higher than for traditional IRAs, SIMPLE IRAs, or Roth IRAs. If you have not been making regular contributions to a traditional IRA for years, you can build up a large balance in a tax-deferred investment account in just a few years by setting up a SEP. You can set up an SEP in a year when you have unusually large profits and substantially reduce your tax liability for that year. In future years, when your income is less, your contributions will be proportionately smaller. You also can terminate the SEP and not make any more contributions to it, leaving the money in it to grow through investment.

The disadvantages of an SEP are that virtually all employees of a company, even those who work for a subsidiary, must be included in the plan, regardless of the amount of time they work for the company, and all employees are fully vested. An employee who works only a few weeks for a company still owns the SEP-IRA even if the contributions for that year are made after the employee leaves the company. After two years, that individual can roll over the SEP into another IRA. A company employing seasonal labor, for example, would not want to contribute to IRAs for each temporary laborer.

SIMPLE IRAs

Any business with fewer than 100 employees who earn at least $5,000 a year can set up a SIMPLE IRA. Under a Savings Incentive Match Plan for Employees (SIMPLE) IRA, employees and employers (including self-employed individuals) both contribute to traditional IRAs set up for each individual employee. SIMPLE IRAs are designed for small employers who do not have another type of retirement plan and are relatively easy to administer. The employer contributes to an IRA for each eligible employee, and employees are able to make pretax contributions from their salaries. An employee has 100 percent ownership of the money in his or her SIMPLE IRA.

As an employer, you can receive a tax deduction for contributions made to a SIMPLE IRA on behalf of your employees, as well as a deduction for the costs of setting up and administering the plan.

The procedure for setting up a SIMPLE IRA is similar to that for setting up a SEP-IRA. You can set up IRAs for all your employees at one financial institution, or allow each employee to set up an IRA at a financial institution he or she chooses. A qualified employee is one who has received at least $5,000 in compensation during any two years preceding the current calendar year and is reasonably expected to receive at least $5,000 during the current calendar year. Employers can choose to use less restrictive criteria to define a qualified employee.

Employees must be notified that they can elect to contribute a salary deduction to an IRA and that the amount of the contribution can be changed each year during a 60-day election period immediately preceding January 1 of a calendar year. An employer may choose to match each employee's contribution up to 3 percent of his or her salary or make a nonelective contribution of 2 percent of each employee's salary.

The financial institution administers individual SIMPLE IRAs; the employer is only responsible for making contributions. The financial institution provides employees with regular statements of their account balances.

The contribution limit for a SIMPLE IRA in 2011 was $11,500 ($14,000 for employees older than 50). Rules and penalties for withdrawals and distributions are the same as for all other traditional IRAs with one exception: if funds are withdrawn within two years of enrolling in a SIMPLE IRA, then the penalty is 25 percent instead of 10 percent.

How to Set Up an IRA

Banks, stockbrokers, and financial institutions of all kinds offer IRAs. They make it easy to set up a new account or roll over a 401(k) plan by making arrangements for you and provide you with regular statements and reports. Often, financial institutions create special IRA mutual funds and investment portfolios to which you can make small, regular contributions. Target date funds, which gradually move your money from high-risk to lower-risk investments as you approach retirement age, are popular. If you want to take a more active role, look for an IRA that lets you select your own investments. Shop around for IRAs with good-quality investment funds and low management costs.

Be sure to keep all the information about your IRA(s) in a safe place where your heirs will be able to find it in case something happens to you. When you open an IRA, you will be asked to fill in a form naming your beneficiaries. Update this information when you are married or divorced or you have a child. Only the beneficiaries listed on your form can inherit your IRA.

If you have a 401(k) plan through your employer

If your online sales business is a sideline and you work for an employer that matches contributions to a 401(k) plan, contribute to the 401(k) plan from your salary at work, and use money from your online sales business for your living expenses. Matching contributions are free money and will increase your retirement savings faster than the investments in an IRA. Your employer is allowed to make matching contributions equal to up to 3 percent of your salary to a 401(k). If you have contributed this amount to your 401(k), and you have more money to put into your savings, put the next $5,000 ($6,000 if you are older than 50) into a traditional IRA or a Roth IRA. Contribute any amounts over that to your 401(k) until you reach the annual contribution limit of $16,500 (in 2010). You are allowed to contribute a maximum of $16,500 (plus an additional $5,500 catch-up contribution if you are 50 or older) to your 401(k) and $5,000 ($6,000 if you are older than 50) to your traditional IRA (in 2010). Depending on your total income, you may be able to deduct only a portion of your IRA contribution from your taxable income, while all of your contributions to a 401(k) are excluded from taxable income.

If your employer does not match 401(k) contributions, look carefully at all your options before deciding where to put your retirement savings. Companies are allowed to set rules for their 401(k) plans that are more restrictive than the rules for IRAs. For example, a company may require that your spouse be listed as your beneficiary and may require your beneficiary to withdraw all the funds from your 401(k) soon after your death instead of allowing him or her to keep the money in the 401(k) and withdraw annual distributions over his or her lifetime. Study the investment options offered by the 401(k) and the fees charged for management and commissions. Some 401(k) plans are better than others; excessive fees and charges can keep your retirement savings from increasing as they should. If your company 401(k) charges high fees or offers mediocre investment choices, then you are better off putting your money in an IRA and choosing your own investments. Some 401(k) plans allow you to "borrow" hardship loans for certain purposes as long as the money is returned within a specified period. You cannot "borrow" from an IRA. Once the money is taken out of an IRA it cannot be replaced, and you must pay income tax on it, plus a penalty for early withdrawal.

When you leave your employment with a company, you can roll over (convert) your 401(k) to a traditional IRA or a Roth IRA. This should be done as soon as possible after you leave the company. If you die unexpectedly, your beneficiaries will be subject to the more flexible IRA rules instead of the stricter requirements of the 401(k). Your beneficiary could be hit with a heavy tax burden if you have a large amount in your 401(k) and it has to be disbursed quickly. Also, you could run into difficulty locating your 401(k) account ten or 20 years down the line if your employer has gone out of business or declared bankruptcy. Look for an IRA with a variety of investment options, low fees, and transparency. Transparency means that all fees and commissions are listed clearly on your statements, instead of being hidden in the costs of individual funds or financial products. You can roll over your 401(k) into an existing IRA or open a new one. Banks and financial institutions offering IRAs typically will handle all the paperwork for you.

Tax-free earnings with a Roth IRA

All your future earnings will be tax-free if you roll your 401(k) over into a Roth IRA. There are no income limits for converting your tax-deferred retirement savings account to a Roth, but you must pay income tax on the amount you are converting.

Investing in Your Online Sales Business with a Self-Directed IRA

Depending on the nature of your online sales business, you might be able to operate it within an IRA so income tax on all your profits is deferred until you cash out the business and withdraw the money from the IRA. This will give you more money to invest in inventory and marketing. A self-directed traditional or Roth IRA is set up to let you manage your own investment account under the administration of a third-party trustee. You can receive a salary for operating your business.

A self-directed IRA can own almost any type of investment, including businesses and real estate, but all of its activities must benefit the IRA rather than the IRA's owner. For example, the IRA owner cannot use property owned by the IRA for personal use, and the IRA cannot buy property from the owner or from members of his or her immediate family. All expenses associated with a business held by an IRA must be paid with money from the IRA. Money and assets in a self-directed IRA cannot be mixed with personal funds.

IRS restrictions on the types of investments an IRA can hold make a self-directed IRA potentially unsuitable for businesses dealing in collectibles such as art, antiques, or coins. Also, all the money withdrawn from an IRA is taxed as personal income. If some of your profits from selling valuable items could have been treated as capital gains, then you will be paying the higher income tax rate instead of the lower capital gains tax. Consult a tax accountant to establish whether you can operate your online sales business as a self-directed IRA without breaking IRS rules. Also, your business must be profitable enough to justify paying the additional fees for administration of a self-directed IRA.

Establishing a self-directed IRA

The "self-directed IRAs" many financial institutions advertise are IRAs that allow you to choose which stocks, bonds, and mutual funds to invest in. A completely self-directed Roth IRA offers the flexibility to invest in many types of assets, including real estate and business ownership. To distinguish themselves, some companies advertise a "truly self-directed IRA," which means they are prepared to handle many types of investments and put you in charge of managing them. An IRA with "checkbook control" is an arrangement that lets you handle the financial transactions associated with your investment under the administration of a third-party trustee.

A self-directed IRA must have both a custodian and a trustee/administrator. The custodian, a bank, credit union, savings and loan, or financial institution holds your account and reports regularly to the IRS but cannot be involved in any investment decisions. A trustee holds your assets, acts on your behalf in certain matters, and is obligated by law to act in your best interests. The administrator does not hold assets, but handles details such as receiving your contributions and executing your instructions regarding transactions. An IRA administrator is typically a company employing a staff of accountants, lawyers, and finance professionals. It might be a small company with a handful of employees or a large firm serving thousands of clients. It is important to choose an administrator that is equipped to handle transactions for your type of business. You do not want to do the extra work of changing administrators later on when your investment plans are under way.

You can find potential administrators by typing "self-directed IRA" in an online search engine, inquiring at banks and brokerages, or asking professionals and friends for recommendations. A company that has been in business for a long time will have an established reputation and a large, experienced staff. On the other hand, a smaller company might offer more personal attention and a faster response to your requests. Inquire if the company is bonded for theft or fraud and insured for errors and omissions. Ask to see the company's annual financial statements, and look for footnotes referring to litigation or payments for legal fees or settlements. A good administrator will have access to experts outside the company who can give legal advice and answer questions when a situation is unclear.

Administrative fees for a typical IRA are less than $100 per year, while fees for a self-directed IRA can range from several hundred to more than $1,000 a year for a $100,000 account, reflecting the additional services provided. A self-directed IRA incurs fees both from the IRA custodian and the administrator. Custodians generally charge a fee for each transaction and might charge an annual fee. A fee-based administrator charges either a flat annual fee or a fee for each service or transaction, in addition to the custodian's fee. An asset-based administrator charges an annual fee based either on the value or the number and type of assets in the IRA. Some administrators charge a flat annual fee along with a fee for each transaction. There might also be a termination fee when you close your account or transfer to another IRA.

Paying fees with outside funds means more money stays in your IRA

Many IRA owners pay IRA administrators' fees with outside funds to preserve as much cash as possible inside the IRA.

The major players

To prevent misuse of the tax benefits offered by an IRA and the manipulation of clients by financial institutions, the IRS has strict rules governing the way that a self-directed IRA can be structured. For example, only a bank or an approved financial entity can hold the assets in your IRA, and it must submit annual reports to the IRS. This financial entity cannot interfere in investment decisions. You are not allowed to carry out transactions directly, such as buying and selling a business or real estate in an IRA; a professional intermediary must do this. Though a custodian might manage an IRA invested in mutual funds, stocks, and bonds, a self-directed IRA typically requires the additional services of an administrator/trustee. The responsibilities of each are different:

- **Custodian**
  Your IRA custodian is the bank or financial institution that holds your IRA account. The custodian is responsible for keeping the accounts and reporting to you and to the IRA. According to IRS rules, an IRA custodian must remain neutral in regard to investment decisions, taking direction from the IRA owner, and not attempting to influence or advise him or her. According to federal law, only a bank, savings and loan, credit union, or an institution or individual who has received approval from the IRS may act as an IRA custodian.

- **Trustee**
  A trustee represents a trust that holds assets on your behalf and has the authority to act on your behalf in certain matters. A trustee is obligated by law to act in your best interests.

- **Administrator**
  An IRA administrator handles the administrative details of an IRA account and acts as an interface between the IRA owner and the custodian or trustee. An administrator does not hold assets or have

fiduciary authority over assets in the IRA. An administrator carries out the process of opening and closing an IRA account; receives contributions; executes rollovers, transfers, and distributions; and conveys the account holder's instructions regarding transactions.

Checkbook control

One of the limitations of a self-directed IRA is that the owner must instruct the IRA custodian to carry out financial transactions on his or her behalf, resulting in delays, extra paperwork, and custodian transactional fees. To get around this difficulty, the owner of a self-directed IRA sets up a LLC that he or she manages and instructs the IRA custodian to invest in it and transfer funds to the LLC bank account. This is known as "checkbook control." The IRA owner has sole signing authority for the bank accounts of the LLC and can carry out financial transactions without the involvement of the IRA custodian. The profits of the LLC go directly to the IRA.

This structure was officially sanctioned by a tax court case, *Swanson v. Commissioner of Internal Revenue, 106 T.C. 76 (1996)*. James Swanson, owner of Swanson's Tools, set up a company called Worldwide to export tools abroad. An IRA set up by James Swanson owned all shares of Worldwide, and the company received commissions for its export sales and paid dividends to the IRA. The IRS characterized this arrangement as "self-dealing" and declared these "prohibited transactions." Swanson appealed, and the court declared that the payment of dividends to the IRA, by a company wholly owned by the IRA, benefited the IRA and did not directly benefit James Swanson. This ruling set a precedent for self-directed IRAs to own a business managed by the IRA owner and receive income from that business without losing their tax-deferred status.

The IRA custodian is a nondiscretionary trustee, which means it does not offer legal or tax advice or ensure that legal requirements are met. The IRA owner is responsible for making sure all codes, regulations, and legal requirements are complied with. It is essential for the owner of a self-directed

IRA who sets up an LLC to seek out the independent advice of accountants, lawyers, and business advisors who are not affiliated with the IRA custodian and who understand the IRS rules concerning IRAs.

Funding a self-directed IRA

The amount available for investment in a self-directed IRA is restricted by annual IRA contribution limits ($5,000 per year, $6,000 if you are older than 50, in 2011). You might have a substantial amount to invest if you are rolling over a 401(k) or other retirement plan, have inherited an IRA, or have already accumulated a substantial IRA balance. Before setting up a self-directed IRA, confirm that the amount in your account will be sufficient for your business. If your business qualifies for a loan, then you can leverage the money in your IRA by having your LLC take out a business loan to be paid back with business income. Your IRA also can buy a partial interest, or partnership, in a company that is otherwise established with outside funds or in collaboration with a spouse or other family member. You will manage the company, but only the IRA's share of the profits can be deposited in the IRA account.

All expenses must be paid from IRA funds

IRS rules do not allow the use of personal funds to pay expenses associated with an investment your IRA owns. If cash is needed to pay for maintenance, supplies, or service charges associated with real estate or a business owned by your IRA, then you must ensure there is enough cash in your IRA account to cover these needs.

Protecting the tax-deferred status of the account

Always consult a CPA or attorney who knows retirement planning and tax law to ensure your IRA investments are structured in a way that does not violate IRA rules. One simple mistake might result in the sudden loss of your IRA's tax benefits. If you engage in a prohibited transaction in connection with your IRA, the account stops being an IRA. The account is treated as though all the assets in it had been distributed to you at their fair market values on the first day of that year. You could end up with a large taxable income for that year and find yourself in a higher tax bracket. If you are younger than 59 ½, you must also pay a 10-percent early withdrawal penalty.

Self-directed IRAs are in particular danger of violating IRS rules regarding prohibited transactions. The IRS stipulates that every transaction in a self-directed IRA must be for the primary benefit of the IRA. The purpose of an IRA is to use tax privileges to generate retirement income for the owner, not to provide concessions or tax breaks to the IRA owner and his or her immediate family. Your IRA custodian, trustee, and administrator also are prohibited from using your IRA for their personal benefit.

You cannot pay yourself a salary from a company your IRA owns unless the company is structured so someone else decides your compensation. You are not allowed to commingle your personal funds with IRA funds or to loan money to your IRA. A business your IRA owns cannot furnish free goods or services to you or your administrator. Income from the business must go straight to the IRA account. That money can be reinvested in your business or invested in other assets as long as it stays within the IRA.

The penalty for a prohibited transaction is the immediate distribution of all assets in the IRA and the loss of its tax-free status

Prohibited transactions

Excerpt from *Internal Revenue Service Publication 590, Traditional IRAs* www.irs.gov/publications/p590/ch01.html#en_US_pub-link10006397.

Generally, a prohibited transaction is any improper use of your traditional IRA account or annuity by you, your beneficiary, or any disqualified person.

Disqualified persons include your fiduciary and members of your family (spouse, ancestor, lineal descendant, and any spouse of a lineal descendant). The following are examples of prohibited transactions with a traditional IRA:

- Borrowing money from it
- Selling property to it
- Receiving unreasonable compensation for managing it
- Using it as security for a loan
- Buying property for personal use (present or future) with IRA funds

Fiduciary

For these purposes, a fiduciary includes anyone who does any of the following:

- Exercises any discretionary authority or discretionary control in managing your IRA or exercises any authority or control in managing or disposing of its assets.

- Provides investment advice to your IRA for a fee or has any authority or responsibility to do so

- Has any discretionary authority or discretionary responsibility in administering your IRA

- Has an effect on an IRA account. Generally, if you or your beneficiary engages in a prohibited transaction in connection with your traditional IRA account at any time during the year, then the account stops being an IRA as of the first day of that year.

- Has an effect on you or your beneficiary. If your account stops being an IRA because you or your beneficiary engaged in a prohibited transaction, then the account is treated as distributing all its assets to you at their fair market values on the first day of the year. If the total   of those values is more than your basis in the IRA, then you will have a taxable gain that is includable in your income.

- Borrows on an annuity contract. If you borrow money against your traditional IRA annuity contract, then you must include in your gross income the fair market value of the annuity contract as of the first day of your tax year. You might have to pay the 10 percent additional tax on early distributions discussed later.

- Pledges an account as security. If you use a part of your traditional IRA account as security for a loan, then that part is treated as a distribution and is included in your gross income. You might have to pay the 10 percent additional tax on early distributions.

CHAPTER 13

What to Do When Things Go Wrong

You complete your tax return for the previous year and find, to your dismay, that you owe several thousand dollars in taxes. April 15 is just two days away, and you do not have enough money to pay the tax you owe. You decide to delay filing your tax return until you can scrape together the funds to pay your taxes. Several months pass, and one day you receive a letter from the IRS informing you that you not only owe taxes but also are accruing penalties. You have not been paying sales tax, and one day you read that your state is cracking down on Internet sales.

You could be in trouble! You discover, too late, that you underpaid quarterly estimated tax for the second quarter of the year. A letter from the IRS arrives, notifying you that you have been selected for a tax audit. What do you do now?

Avoid Trouble by Timely Reporting

You can avert many tax problems by filing your returns on time or contacting the IRS for information and assistance. According to Section 7201 of the Internal Revenue Code (IRC), it is a federal crime for anyone willfully to attempt to evade or defeat the payment of federal income taxes. Tax evasion is a felony punishable with up to a five-year prison sentence and/or fines up to $100,000. Filing a false return (providing wrong information on a tax return) is also a felony, punishable by up to three years in prison and/or up to $100,000 in fines. Not filing a tax return at all is a misdemeanor, punishable by a maximum of one year in prison and/or fines totaling up to $25,000 for each year you failed to file. Wouldn't it be easier to file on time?

If your tax return is not ready by the April 15 deadline, you can get a six-month extension by filing *Form 4868, Application for Automatic Extension of Time To File U.S. Individual Income Tax Return* (**www.irs.gov/pub/irs-pdf/f4868.pdf**) by the due date for filing your calendar year return (usually April 15) or fiscal year return. More information can be found in IRS *Publication 17: Your Federal Income Tax* (**www.irs.gov/pub/irs-pdf/p17.pdf**).

You also do not have to pay the entire amount of tax on April 15. You can arrange to pay your tax debt in installments. If you owe $25,000 or less in taxes, penalties, and interest, you can fill out an Online Payment Agreement (OPA) (**www.irs.gov/individuals/article/0,,id=149373,00.html**). You also can mail in a paper request form, *Form 9465: Installment Agree-*

ment Request (**www.irs.gov/pub/irs-pdf/f9465.pdf**). If you owe more than $25,000, then you might still be able to arrange installment payments, but you will have to fill out *Collection Information Statement, Form 433F* (**www.irs.gov/individuals/article/0,,id=149373,00.html**) and send it in along with Form 9465. You will be notified in writing whether your payment plan has been accepted.

If taxes are not paid and no effort is made to pay them, then the IRS can ask a taxpayer to take action to pay the taxes, such as selling or mortgaging any assets owned or getting a loan. If effort is still not made to pay the bill or make other payment arrangements, then the IRS could take more serious enforced collection action, such as levying bank accounts, wages, or other income, or taking other assets. A Notice of Federal Tax Lien could be filed that might have a detrimental effect on a taxpayer's credit standing.

If You Have Not Filed a Tax Return

It is never too late to file a tax return. File all past due returns now, even if you cannot pay the taxes, to avoid additional penalties and interest. If you do not file your taxes and fail to contact the IRS, then the IRS will file a substitute return for you, which will not include any additional exemptions or expenses you might be entitled to and might overstate your real tax liability. Once the tax is assessed, the IRS will start the collection process, which can include placing a levy on wages or bank accounts or filing a federal tax lien against your property.

If You Have Not Paid Your Taxes

The federal government really wants its money and will go to great lengths to get it. If you have not paid your taxes, or if you cannot pay, there are several options.

If you are unable to pay all taxes due on the bill, then you are encouraged to pay as much as possible now to lessen the amount of penalties and interest owed. Call the number or write to the address on your tax bill, or visit the nearest IRS office to explain your situation.

You can avoid some of the interest incurred by an installment plan by entering into a short-term agreement to pay in full within 60 or 120 days.

If you cannot pay any of your tax debt, the IRS may allow you to delay payment temporarily until your financial situation improves. Penalties and interest will continue to accrue until the full amount is paid.

Offer in Compromise

An offer in compromise (OIC) is an agreement between a taxpayer and the IRS that settles the taxpayer's tax liabilities for less than the full amount owed. Unless there are special circumstances, an offer will not be accepted if the IRS believes the liability can be paid in full as a lump sum or through a payment agreement.

In most cases, the IRS will not accept an OIC unless the amount offered by the taxpayer is equal to or greater than the reasonable collection potential (RCP). The RCP is how the IRS measures the taxpayer's ability to pay and includes the value that can be realized from the taxpayer's assets, such as real property, automobiles, bank accounts, and other property. The RCP also includes anticipated future income, less certain amounts allowed for basic living expenses.

Tax debts cannot be "settled for pennies on the dollar"

Beware of companies that promise to settle your tax debt for "pennies on the dollar" through the offer in compromise program. There is no easy way out of a tax debt. You can negotiate your own OIC directly with the IRS; you do not need assistance from a debt settlement company that will only charge you additional fees.

The IRS will accept an OIC on one of three grounds: there is doubt that the taxpayer could ever pay the full amount of tax liability owed within the remainder of the statutory period for collection; there is a legitimate possibility that a mistake was made in assessing the tax bill, such as a misinterpretation of the law or unexamined evidence; or the taxpayer can demonstrate that the collection of the tax would create an economic hardship or would be unfair and inequitable.

Requesting a Waiver for Estimated Quarterly Tax Penalties

If you have underpaid quarterly estimated taxes or have made late payments, then you can request the IRS to waive the penalties under certain circumstances. These circumstances include not being able to pay because a casualty, accident, natural disaster, or other unusual event interrupted your business operations. Another circumstance is if you retired (at age 62) or became disabled during the year. You will need to use *Form 2210* to request the waiver and attach it to your tax return along with a statement explaining why you are seeking the waiver and supporting documentation, such as retirement documents or police reports. Instructions for requesting a waiver are found in *IRS Publication 505: Tax Withholding and Estimated Tax* (**http://www.irs.gov/pub/irs-pdf/p505.pdf**).

If your business is in a federally declared disaster area, do not fill out a *Form 1022* to request a waiver. The IRS automatically postpones tax deadlines for anyone with an address in the disaster area, and uses ZIP codes to identify eligible taxpayers. If your business uses an accountant or other professional service within the federally declared disaster area, or if your books and records are located there, then you also qualify for a waiver. Call the IRS disaster hotline at (866) 562-5227 to identify yourself as eligible for this relief.

Taxpayer Advocate Service

The Taxpayer Advocate Service (TAS) is an independent body within the IRS that acts on the taxpayer's behalf. It assists taxpayers who are experiencing economic harm, such as not being able to afford necessities, such as food, housing, and transportation, and taxpayers who need help resolving problems with the IRS. The service is free, confidential, and personal. You might be eligible for TAS assistance if you have tried to resolve your problem through normal channels without success or if you believe that an IRS procedure is not working as it should. If you qualify, then an advocate will be assigned to work with you until the problem is resolved. There is a taxpayer advocate in every state. Contact information can be found in *Pub. 1546, Taxpayer Advocate Service – Your Voice at the IRS*, and on the IRS website (**www.irs.gov/advocate**). The toll-free number is (877) 777-4778.

If You Are Selected for an Audit

Your online sales business activities, by their nature, might attract attention from the IRS. Only 2 percent to 4 percent of all tax returns are audited, but there is always a possibility that yours will be among them. The IRS selects potential candidates for audits with software programs that compile data from the tax returns of similar taxpayers and from previous years and identify those with abnormally high amounts for certain deductibles or consistently low profits. Some things that draw attention are excessive automobile expenses, multiple vehicles used by a small business, large deductions for interest on loans, and abnormal amounts spent on travel and entertainment. Other reasons why you might be selected for an audit include a relationship with another taxpayer who is being audited, reports from informers, or being part of a group that has been singled out for auditing, such as freelance consultants.

If you have followed the suggestions in Chapter 2 and maintained accurate records and receipts to back up all your expenses, then you have no reason to worry. You can be almost certain, however, that you will end up paying a higher tax bill after the audit. The IRS only audits accounts when it is reasonably certain that it will be able to recover additional revenue. There are likely to be expenses or deductions that you will have to reduce or delete on your tax return, increasing your taxable income for the year.

There are four types of IRS audits:

Correspondence audit: You receive a letter from the IRS Service Center asking you to send in copies of your canceled checks and/or receipts to verify deductions on your return.

Office audit: You receive a letter questioning specific items on your tax return and asking you to bring certain documents to the local IRS office to be examined by the auditor. A small sole proprietorship is most likely to be subjected to this type of audit. Submit only the required documents — do not offer additional information unless it is asked for. If you do not understand your taxes or feel uncertain about the outcome, then have your accountant accompany you or represent you.

Field audit: The business owner receives a personal telephone call from an IRS agent, notifying him or her that the tax return has been selected for audit. The agent will make an appointment to come to your place of business to examine your records and interview the principal officers. Partnerships and corporations typically are subjected to field audits. You should have an accountant or tax professional represent you during a field audit because the IRS representative will be casting around for additional evidence of wrongdoing. Ideally, the meeting can take place in the accountant's office instead of at your business.

Taxpayer Compliance Measurement Program (TCMP) audit: The main purpose of a TCMP audit is to update the data used by the IRS in its analysis programs. Every line of your tax return is audited, and you must supply documentation for all your deductions, not just a few items. This can be time consuming.

You can choose to meet with the auditor yourself, have an accountant or tax professional accompany you, or have a professional represent you. Even though you will have to spend money on professional fees, it is often a good idea to have someone represent you. A representative protects you from having to directly answer awkward questions. A professional speaks the same language as the IRS, is less emotional, and better able to negotiate with the IRS agent.

If you do choose to handle the audit yourself:

- Stay calm.

- Organize your documents and information before you start.

- Do everything in a timely manner, to show that you have nothing to hide.

- Give the IRS agent only the documents or information asked for, no more and no less.

- Give brief, honest answers to questions.

- Avoid idle chatter; anything you say gives the IRS agent more information about you.

- Never give the IRS the only copy of a document, and do not leave your original records with the IRS. Insist on getting copies of their files and copies of any document you sign.

- Do not sign anything you do not understand. You can ask your accountant to review the document first.

At the end of the audit, the IRS agent will present you with a bill for any unpaid taxes and penalties. You can choose to sign it or to appeal. If you think the bill is in error, the IRS agent should explain the appeal process.

Free Tax Help

All IRS forms, publications, articles, and rulings are available to the public on the IRS website (**www.irs.gov**). Many of them are listed in the *Useful Websites* at the end of this book. You also can find clarification and helpful information on the websites and blogs of countless professionals and organizations by typing your question into an Internet search engine.

Free help in preparing your tax return is available nationwide from IRS-trained volunteers. The Volunteer Income Tax Assistance (VITA) program helps low-income taxpayers and the Tax Counseling for the Elderly (TCE) program assists taxpayers age 60 and older with their taxes. To find the nearest VITA or TCE site, call (800) 829-1040. AARP offers the Tax-Aide counseling program in conjunction with TCE. Call (888) 227-7669, or visit AARP's website at **www.aarp.org/money/taxaide**.

Unpaid Sales Tax

Money that you collect as sales tax is never your money. It belongs to your state, and you are responsible for transferring it in a timely manner. If you have fallen behind on your sales tax payments and do not have the money to pay, then you are still held responsible. When you fail to file sales tax returns and make payment arrangements, you will face additional interest, penalties, liens, levies, and audits. Eventually, the state will cancel your sales tax license, which will make it illegal for you to do business. File the delinquent sales tax returns right away, and contact your state tax authority to make payment arrangements. Like the IRS, state taxing authorities offer installment plans and even compromise offers.

Most states charge a late fee for failing to file a sales tax return, even if you have no sales tax to report. If you go out of business and late fees pile up because you forgot to deactivate your sales tax license, then you might be able to get the late penalties waived by calling the state taxing authority and explaining the situation.

CHAPTER 14

Ten Biggest Tax Mistakes

The previous chapters have demonstrated that there is more to a successful online business than selling a lot of merchandise. You must pay taxes on your profits, and any strategy that legitimately reduces those taxes is money earned. When you sell through an online marketplace, there is an electronic trail for every transaction. You cannot hide how much income you are making from your sales. Many individuals who start up small businesses from their homes are unaware of tax laws and inadvertently make mistakes that increase their tax bills or land them in legal trouble. Avoid unpleasant surprises by reviewing home business owners' ten biggest tax mistakes:

1. **Failure to register your business.**

   Your business is not legal if you do not comply with all state and local registration requirements and zoning regulations. You cannot claim you are a business and deduct business expenses if you are not a legitimate business.

2. **Not keeping receipts.**

   It is easy to clear out your wallet and throw out the receipts for that ream of printer paper you bought at Walmart or the box of pens from Staples®. How are you going to remember all those little expenses when it is time to do your taxes? If the IRS selects you for an audit, then you will be required to produce receipts for all your business expenses. Make a habit of filing away receipts as soon as you come back to your office and recording your expenses regularly.

3. **Mixing business and personal assets.**

   To qualify as business assets, computers and other equipment must be dedicated primarily to business use. Your home office must also be a dedicated space. When you sell a personal item that has been in your family for years, the profit can be taxed at a lower capital gains rate instead of the income tax rate charged on business income. Mixing personal and business assets could cost you a tax deduction or cause you to be taxed at a higher rate.

4. **Taking a deduction from business income for personal compensation and time spent working in the business.**

   You are not allowed to count the hours you spend operating your business as a business expense.

5. **Overlooking self-employment tax.**

   Do not forget that you must pay the employer's half of Social Security and Medicare tax — more than 15 percent of your income in most years. That is a substantial amount of money that must be paid to the IRS on a quarterly basis. If you ignore it, then you could end up with an unexpected tax liability and pay penalties and interest.

6. **Ignoring quarterly income tax payments.**

   The U.S. tax system is pay-as-you-go; a self-employed individual is required to pay income tax at four regular intervals throughout the year. Underpaying or failing to make regular payments adds penalties and interest to your tax liability.

7. **Not paying sales tax.**

   Many states require you to collect sales tax on retail sales. That money belongs to the state and must be remitted regularly. Failure to report and pay sales tax will result in penalties and interest and eventually could cause you to lose your sales tax license.

8. **Not taking full advantage of tax-advantaged retirement accounts.**

   Tax-advantaged retirement accounts let you either defer income tax and invest more money or withdraw tax-free earnings when you retire. Both of these privileges result in considerably more money for your retirement. The amount you can contribute each year is limited to $5,000 or $6,000. Make the most of these tax benefits by contributing every year. The earlier you start contributing, the more time your money will have to grow.

9. **Failing to file tax returns.**

   Taxes will not go away if you do not file your tax returns on time. Instead, you eventually could be charged with tax evasion, a felony punishable with jail time and fines. In the meantime, the IRS will file your returns for you, leaving out many of the credits and deductions you might qualify for, and it will come after you to collect the debt. Even if you cannot pay, file your tax returns on time and communicate with the IRS to resolve your difficulty.

10. **Falsifying information.**

    It might be tempting to write off a family vacation trip or a new car as a business expense, but the computer software used by the IRS will detect unusually large deductions. You could become the subject of an audit and end up paying penalties and interest in addition to the income tax you owe. Do not report any business expenses that you cannot back up with solid evidence.

Conclusion

Y ou probably did not realize that operating even a simple online sales business could be so complicated. Your financial success depends not only on your ability to find and market good products but also on your ability to organize and maintain accurate financial records and your familiarity with the tax code. By planning and managing your expenses and assets well, you can shave hundreds of dollars off your tax bill and be able to keep more of your money. Up-to-date records allow you to monitor your business and see exactly how much profit you are making, how you can improve your sales, and what practices are causing you to lose money.

The Internal Revenue Code might seem to be a monstrous behemoth, but its many rules and regulations are based on statistical analysis and are born from attempts to keep the burden on individual taxpayers reasonable while preventing abuse and implementing government initiatives to stimulate the economy and reduce energy consumption. Tax preparation and accounting software have taken some of the pain out of computing taxes and made it easier to comprehend the effect of various actions on your tax bill. Accurately reporting your income and your expenses will probably place you just about where you belong in the tax structure and allow you to take advantage of all the credits and deductions legally available to you.

As various chapters have pointed out, ignoring tax laws or falsifying information can land you in deep financial and legal trouble. Ignorance is not an excuse. Information is available everywhere — in official IRS publications and articles, business magazines, on the Internet in forums, blogs, and articles, from accountants and tax professionals, and from fellow online merchants. The more you understand about tax laws, the better you will be able to navigate them. The many topics in this book are only an introduction to many of the topics that may concern you. Take the information that applies to your particular business and your personal circumstances, and keep asking questions until you feel confident that you fully understand it. I wish you many years of success!

Useful Websites and References

Bookkeeping

IRS Publication 583: Starting a Business and Keeping Records.
IRS.gov. **www.irs.gov/pub/irs-pdf/p583.pdf.**

Microsoft Excel templates.
http://office.microsoft.com/en-us/templates#.

Small Business Administration free online classes.
www.sba.gov/content/recordkeeping.

SBA local branches. **www.sba.gov/content/find-local-sba-office.**

Data Storage

Free Tutorials Baycon Group. **www.baycongroup.com/el0.htm.**

Microsoft. **http://office.microsoft.com/en-us/excel-help.**

Mozy. **http://mozy.com**.

SugarSync. **www.sugarsync.com**.

Business Plans

"How to Write a Business Plan." Small Business Association (SBA). **www.sba.gov/smallbusinessplanner/plan/writeabusinessplan/ index.html**.

Family Business

Election for Husband and Wife Unincorporated Businesses. **www.irs.gov/businesses/small/article/0,,id=177376,00.html**.

Husband and Wife Business. IRS.gov. **www.irs.gov/businesses/small/article/0,,id=97732,00.html**.

Inventory

IRS Publication 538: Accounting Periods and Methods. **www.irs.gov/pub/irs-pdf/p538.pdf**.

IRS Publication 551: Basis of Assets. **www.irs.gov/pub/irs-pdf/p551.pdf**.

IRS Publication 561. Determining the Value of Donated Property. **www.irs.gov/publications/p561/index.html**.

"Tax Laws and Issues for Online Auction Sellers." **www.irs.gov/ businesses/small/industries/article/0,,id=202941,00.html**.

"Tax Tips for Online Auction Sellers." **www.irs.gov/businesses/small/ industries/article/0,,id=202939,00.html**.

"Ten Important Facts About Capital Gains and Losses." IRS Tax Tip 2011-35. Feb. 18, 2011. **www.irs.gov/newsroom/article/0,,id=106799,00.html**.

Licenses and Permits

"Auctioneer and Auction Boards Guide." A1 Auctions.
www.a1auctions.com/licensing.htm.

"Auctioneering Regulations." EBay Main Street.
www.ebaymainstreet.com/policy-papers/auctioneering-regulations.

SBA.gov's Business Licenses and Permits Search Tool.
www.sba.gov/content/search-business-licenses-and-permits.

Logo Design

Guru Corporation's LogoSnap.com. **www.logosnap.com**.

HP's LogoMaker. **http://logomaker.com**.

Online Marketplaces

EBay. **www.eBay.com**.

EBay Feedback rules.
http://pages.ebay.com/help/policies/feedback-ov.html.

EBay's list of restricted and prohibited items.
http://pages.ebay.com/help/policies/items-ov.html.

Etsy.com. **www.etsy.com**.

Sales Tax

Amazon.
www.amazon.com/gp/help/customer/display.html?nodeId=468512.

"Do You Have to Pay Sales Tax on Internet Purchases?" Findlaw.com.
**http://smallbusiness.findlaw.com/business-operations/internet/
internet-taxes.html**.

EBay. **http://pages.ebay.com/help/pay/checkout-tax-table.html**. **http://pages.ebay.com/help/sell/contextual/inframe/sales-tax.html**.

EBay: *Using a tax table* (to set up sales tax). **http://pages.ebay.com/help/pay/checkout-tax-table.html**.

Etsy.com. **www.etsy.com/storque/seller-handbook/tax-tips-everything-you-need-to-know-about-sales-tax-10963**.

Main Street Fairness Act. **www.opencongress.org/bill/111-h5660/show**.

State Taxing Authorities-Federation of Tax Administrators. **www.taxadmin.org/fta/link**.

Streamlined Sales Tax Project (SSUTA). **www.streamlinedsalestax.org**.

Summary of sales tax requirements by state online. Outright.com. **http://education.outright.com/state-sales-tax-rates-and-requirements-by-state**.

Self-Employment Tax

If You Are Self-Employed. SSA Publication No. 05-10022. January 2011. ICN 454900. **www.ssa.gov/pubs/10022.html**.

IRS Schedule SE (Form 1040): Self-Employment Tax. **www.irs.gov/pub/irs-pdf/f1040sse.pdf**.

"Topic 554 — Self-Employment Tax." **www.irs.gov/taxtopics/tc554.html**.

Shipping

FedEx. **http://fedex.com**

U.S. Postal Service. **www.USPS.com**.

Social Security and Retirement

AARP. **www.aarp.org/work/social-security**.

American Institute of Certified Public Accountants (AICPA). **www.aicpa.org/InterestAreas/PersonalFinancialPlanning/Resources/ConsumerContent/FindaCPAPFSNearYou/Pages/default.aspx**.

"Annual Statistical Supplement, Social Security (Old-Age, Survivors, and Disability Insurance) Program Description and Legislative History." SSA Office of Retirement and Disability Policy. **www.ssa.gov/policy/docs/statcomps/supplement/2010/oasdi.html**.

Chartered Financial Analysts Institute (CFA Institute). **www.cfainstitute.org**.

Financial Planning Association (or FPA). **www.fpanet.org**.

National Association of Personal Financial Advisors (NAPFA). **www.napfa.org**.

Social Security Administration (SSA) Business Services Online. **www.ssa.gov/bso/bsowelcome.htm**.

Social Security Benefits Planner. **www.ssa.gov/planners.**

State Taxes

Chart of Business Taxes by State: "State Tax Treatment of LLCs and LLPs — 2011 Update." **www.babc.com/files/Publication/5ac35bb5-2520-4e20-a88f-99bb519612fd/Presentation/PublicationAttachment/2c86a094-89f2-4729-831f-a617a7eaa89e/Ely.pdf**.

Taxes

"Alternative Minimum Tax (AMT) Assistant for Individuals." **www.irs.gov/businesses/small/article/0,,id=150703,00.html**.

American Institute of CPAs (AICPA).
www.aicpa.org/ForThePublic/FindACPA/Pages/FindACPA.aspx.

"Capitalization Period of Direct and Indirect Costs."
www.irs.gov/businesses/small/industries/article/0,,id=97675,00.html.

Cost Segregation Audit Technique Guide — Chapter 6.1 Uniform Capitalization. **www.irs.gov/businesses/article/0,,id=134361,00.html**.

CPAdirectory.com™. **www.cpadirectory.com**.

"Deductible Taxes." **www.irs.gov/taxtopics/tc503.html**.

"Do You Need an EIN?" IRS.
www.irs.gov/businesses/small/article/0,,id=97872,00.html.

Federal tax bracket calculator. efile.com.
www.efile.com/tax-service/tax-calculator/tax-brackets.

File W-2 forms for your employees. Social Security Administration (SSA) Business Services Online. **www.ssa.gov/bso/bsowelcome.htm**.

Form W-12, IRS Paid Preparer Tax Identification Number Application. **www.irs.gov/pub/irs-pdf/fw12.pdf**.

Income Tax Rates. efile.com.
www.efile.com/tax-service/tax-calculator/tax-brackets.

IRS Free File tax preparation companies if your AGI is less than $58,000 (2010). **http://apps.irs.gov/app/freeFile/jsp/index.jsp?ck**.

IRS Free File Fillable Forms.
www.freefilefillableforms.com/FFA/Gateway/FED.htm.

"Is it too Good to be True? Home-Based Business Tax Avoidance Schemes." Headliner Volume 295. IRS. May 5, 2010.
www.irs.gov/businesses/small/article/0,,id=222401,00.html.

McCormally, Kevin. Most Overlooked Tax Deductions. Kiplinger. com. December 2010. **www.kiplinger.com/features/archives/the-mostoverlooked-tax-deductions.html**.

"One-Year Rule For Prepaid Expenses." Peter Shannon & Co. **http://petershannonco.com/resources/taxtopics/oneyearrule**.

Online Payment Agreement (OPA). **www.irs.gov/individuals/article/0,,id=149373,00.html**.

PTIN registration. **www.irs.gov/taxpros/article/0,,id=210909,00.html**.

Social Security Administration (SSA). **www.socialsecurity.gov**.

"Standard Mileage Rates." **www.irs.gov/taxpros/article/0,,id=156624,00.html**.

"Tax Tips for Online Auction Sellers." **www.irs.gov/businesses/small/industries/article/0,,id=202939,00.html**.

"Tax Laws and Issues for Online Auction Sellers." **www.irs.gov/businesses/small/industries/article/0,,id=202941,00.html**.

"Tips on Tax Deductions for Charitable Contributions." Lectlaw.com. **www.lectlaw.com/files/tax13.htm**.

U.S. Citizenship and Immigration Services Form 274, Handbook for Employers. **www.uscis.gov/files/nativedocuments/m-274.pdf**.

Where to File Paper Tax Returns — With or Without a Payment. **www.irs.gov/file/index.html**.

WorldWideWebTax™. **www.wwwebtax.com**.

Taxes: IRS Publications and Articles

Cost Segregation Audit Technique Guide — Chapter 6.1 Uniform Capitalization. **www.irs.gov/businesses/article/0,,id=134361,00.html**.

"Election for Husband and Wife Unincorporated Businesses." **www.irs.gov/businesses/small/article/0,,id=177376,00.html**.

"Energy Incentives for Individuals in the American Recovery and Reinvestment Act." **www.irs.gov/newsroom/article/0,,id=206875,00.html**.

General ITIN Information. **www.irs.gov/individuals/article/0,,id=222209,00.html**.

If You Are Self-Employed. SSA Publication No. 05-10022, January 2011, ICN 454900. **www.ssa.gov/pubs/10022.html**.

Instructions for Forms W-2 and W-3 (2011): Wage and Tax Statement and Transmittal of Wage and Tax Statements. **www.irs.gov/instructions/iw2w3/index.html**.

"Inventory — Manufacturing Tax Tips." **www.irs.gov/businesses/small/industries/article/0,,id=100355,00.html**.

IRS e-News Subscriptions. **www.irs.gov/newsroom/content/0,,id=103381,00.html**.

IRS Publication 15. Cat. No. 10000W. (Circular E), Employer's Tax Guide. **www.irs.gov/pub/irs-pdf/p15.pdf**.

IRS *Publication 17: Your Federal Income Tax.* **www.irs.gov/pub/irs-pdf/p17.pdf**.

IRS Topic 424 — 401(k) Plans. **www.irs.gov/taxtopics/tc424.html**.

IRS Publication 501: Exemptions, Standard Deduction and Filing Information. **www.irs.gov/pub/irs-pdf/p501.pdf**.

IRS Publication 505: Tax Withholding and Estimated Tax.
www.irs.gov/pub/irs-pdf/p505.pdf.

IRS Publication 523: Selling Your Home.
www.irs.gov/publications/p523/index.html.

IRS Publication 526: Charitable Contributions.
www.irs.gov/pub/irs-pdf/p526.pdf.

IRS Publication 535: Business Expenses.
www.irs.gov/businesses/small/article/0,,id=109807,00.html.

IRS Publication 538: Accounting Periods and Methods.
www.irs.gov/pub/irs-pdf/p538.pdf.

IRS Publication 544: Sales and Other Dispositions of Assets.
www.irs.gov/publications/p544/index.html.

IRS Publication 550: Investment Income and Expenses.
www.irs.gov/pub/irs-pdf/p550.pdf.

IRS Publication 551: Basis of Assets. **www.irs.gov/pub/irs-pdf/p551.pdf.**

IRS Publication 561: Determining the Value of Donated Property.
www.irs.gov/pub/irs-pdf/p561.pdf.

IRS Publication 587: Business Use of Your Home.
www.irs.gov/pub/irs-pdf/p587.pdf.

IRS Publication 910, IRS Guide to Free Tax Services Reporting Auction Income and the Tax Gap. IRS FS-2007-23, September 2007.
www.irs.gov/newsroom/article/0,,id=174478,00.html.

IRS Publication 946: How to Depreciate Property.
www.irs.gov/pub/irs-pdf/p946.pdf.

IRS Publication 1635: Understanding Your EIN.
www.irs.gov/pub/irs-pdf/p1635.pdf.

IRS Publication 1779: Independent Contractor or Employee.
www.irs.gov/pub/irs-pdf/p1779.pdf.

IRS Workbook on Reporting Cash Payments of Over $10,000.
www.irs.gov/businesses/small/article/0,,id=159755,00.html.

Section179.org.
www.section179.org/section_179_vehicle_deductions.html.

"Small Business and Self-Employed Tax Center — Your Small Business Advantage." **www.irs.gov/businesses/small/index.html**.

"Ten Important Facts About Capital Gains and Losses." IRS Tax Tip 2011-35. Feb.18, 2011. **www.irs.gov/newsroom/article/0,,id=106799,00.html**.

U.S. Citizenship and Immigration Services Form 274, Handbook for Employers. **www.uscis.gov/files/form/m-274.pdf**.

Tax Forms

Collection Information Statement, Form 433F.
www.irs.gov/individuals/article/0,,id=149373,00.html.

EIN — IRS Form SS-4. **www.irs.gov/pub/irs-pdf/iss4.pdf**.

Form 1099-B Proceeds from Broker and Barter Exchange Transactions.
www.irs.gov/pub/irs-pdf/f1099b.pdf.

Form 8283. **www.irs.gov/pub/irs-pdf/f8283.pdf**.

Form 9465: Request for Installment Agreement.
www.irs.gov/pub/irs-pdf/f9465.pdf.

Form SS-8, Determination of Worker Status for Purposes of Federal Employment Taxes and Income Tax Withholding.
www.irs.gov/pub/irs-pdf/fss8.pdf.

Instructions for IRS Form 1040. **www.irs.gov/pub/irs-pdf/i1040.pdf**.

IRS Form 941 Employer's QUARTERLY Federal Tax Return.
www.irs.gov/pub/irs-pdf/f941.pdf.

IRS Form 970, Application To Use LIFO Inventory Method.
www.irs.gov/pub/irs-pdf/f970.pdf.

IRS Form 1099-MISC. **www.irs.gov/pub/irs-pdf/f1099msc.pdf.**
Note: You must obtain a hard copy of the form for filing purposes.

IRS Form 1128: Application to Adopt, Change or Retain a Tax Year.
www.irs.gov/pub/irs-pdf/f1128.pdf.

IRS Form 2210, Underpayment of Estimated Tax by Individuals, Estates, and Trusts. **www.irs.gov/pub/irs-pdf/f2210.pdf.**

IRS Form 3115: Application for Change in Accounting Method.
www.irs.gov/pub/irs-pdf/f3115.pdf.

IRS Form 4684: Casualties and Thefts.
www.irs.gov/pub/irs-pdf/f4684.pdf.

IRS Form 6251: Alternative Minimum Tax—Individuals.
www.irs.gov/pub/irs-pdf/f6251.pdf.

IRS Form 8829: Expenses for Business Use of Your Home.
www.irs.gov/pub/irs-pdf/f8829.pdf.

IRS Form 8888: Direct Deposit of Refund to More Than One Account.
www.irs.gov/pub/irs-pdf/f8888.pdf.

IRS Form W-7, IRS Application for Individual Taxpayer Identification Number. **www.irs.gov/pub/irs-pdf/iw7.pdf.**

IRS Schedule A (Form 1040): Itemized Deductions.
www.irs.gov/pub/irs-pdf/f1040sa.pdf.

IRS Schedule SE (Form 1040): Self-Employment Tax.
www.irs.gov/pub/irs-pdf/f1040sse.pdf.

Order official IRS forms online. **www.irs.gov/businesses/ page/0,,id=23108,00.html,** or call (800) TAX-FORM (800-829-3676).

Schedule C: Profit or Loss from Business. **www.irs.gov/pub/irs-pdf/i1040sc.pdf.**

Schedule D: Capital Gains and Losses. **www.irs.gov/pub/irs-pdf/f1040sd.pdf.**

Trading Assistants

EBay Trading Assistants. **http://ebaytradingassistant.com.**

iSold It. **http://877isoldit.com/products-services/auction-services.asp.**

Troubleshooting Taxes

AARP Tax-Aide counseling program. Call (888) 227-7669, or visit **www.aarp.org/money/taxaide.**

Pub. 1546, Taxpayer Advocate Service — Your Voice at the IRS. **www.irs.gov/pub/irs-pdf/p1546.pdf.**

Tax Counseling for the Elderly (TCE) program for taxpayers age 60 and older. To find the nearest VITA or TCE site, call (800) 829-1040.

Taxpayer Advocate Service. **www.irs.gov/advocate**.

Volunteer Income Tax Assistance (VITA) program for low-income taxpayers.

Websites and Domain Names

InterNIC. **www.internic.net/whois.html**.

GoDaddy.com. **www.godaddy.com.**

Network Solutions. **www.networksolutions.com.**

Business Plan Example for Internet

Essential elements:

1. Executive summary
2. Market analysis
3. Company description
4. Organization and management
5. Marketing and sales management
6. Services and products to be offered
7. Financials
8. Funding requests (if asking for loan)

This business plan is just an example. Your specific plan must reflect your needs, marketing conditions, funding, and the advice you receive from your attorney and accountant.

Executive summary

Shuz N'Bags is an Internet sales business selling quality secondhand and vintage shoes and handbags. It is a qualified joint venture owned and operated by Mr. John Smith and Mrs. Mabel Smith from their home in Applebee, Wisconsin. Shuz N'Bags began operation in October 2008 and realized $10,000 in sales during 2009. During 2010, due to a revival of interest in classic designer handbags, sales more than doubled to $24,000. Sales are strong in 2011, and Shuz N'Bags plans to expand its merchandise selection to include vintage and designer hats.

The business acquires secondhand shoes and bags at auctions, estate sales, thrift stores, and garage sales. It also receives items from clients and sells them on commission. John and Mabel Smith do all of the buying, cataloging, packing, and shipping themselves. They require only occasional assistance from a professional Web designer to upgrade their online store and the services of a part-time bookkeeper. Shuz N'Bags sells merchandise on eBay, Etsy, and Amazon as well as on its own website. Advertising is done through keywords and ad buys, but the business relies mostly on search engines to attract customers for individual items.

Market analysis

Shuz N'Bags customers are primarily women between the ages of 18 and 60 who like vintage clothing or are interested in designer handbags and shoes. A small number of men buy men's shoes and high-end sneakers. Most of Shuz N'Bags customers are in the U.S. and Canada, but about 15 percent are willing to pay the extra shipping costs to have a unique item shipped to the U.K., Australia, Germany, and Latin America. There is potential to expand in these markets if the product descriptions can be translated into Spanish and German. Shuz N'Bags customers are computer-savvy, participate in social networks and blogs, and share information with their friends.

Company description

Shuz N'Bags is a sole proprietorship treated as a qualified joint venture for tax purposes. The owners and operators are John and Mabel Smith.

Organization and management

Shuz N'Bags is headquartered in the home of John and Mabel Smith, at 3606 Venture Way, Applebee, Wisconsin. John Smith has 25 years of experience as a marketing executive, and Mabel Smith has a degree in fashion design from Phoenix University. A website designer and a bookkeeper are employed as part-time contractors, and John and Mabel Smith's daughter and son occasionally assist in filling orders.

Marketing

Because the items are all unique, the descriptions in the catalog listing are the most important factor in selling them. Customers find items by using online search engines. Mabel also maintains a website and blog about vintage clothing and the history of fashion on which new items are featured, and 30 percent of sales are to return customers. A monthly Shuz N'Bags e-mail newsletter gets a good response from customers. Shuz N'Bags purchases featured listings in online marketplaces for its more valuable items and occasionally buys Google ads and featured listings for very specific keywords.

Products

John and Mabel Smith travel extensively in the U.S. and Canada to find quality used shoes and bags. They buy at auctions, estate sales, thrift stores, garage sales, and consignment shops. They have arrangements with several consignment and vintage clothing stores to sell high-end items on commission. The quality and condition of each item is carefully documented in its catalog listing, and Shuz N'Bags has a no-return policy.

All sales are final unless the item is damaged during shipping. Since the wedding of Prince William generated renewed interest in designer hats, Shuz N'Bags has begun experimenting with vintage and designer headwear.

Financials

Make your financial projections for your first three years. Base your estimates on solid information and market conditions.

First, make a column of all of the products you plan to sell and forecast sales for them.

PRODUCT	2011	2012	2013
Shoes	$10,500	$20,000	$20,500
Handbags	$22,000	$35,000	$50,000
Hats	$7,000	$20,000	$30,000
COSTS			
Shoes	$1,500	$2,000	$3,000
Handbags	$3,000	$5,000	$10,000
Hats	$700	$2,500	$5,000
Storage rental	$300	$400	$500
Phone	$600	$625	$700
Insurance	$2,000	$2,100	$2,200
Ad/marketing	$1,000	$1,500	$2,000
Fuel	$1,800	$2,000	$2,000
Travel	$2,000	$2,000	$2,000

It is important that you make a good faith effort to predict your costs. Your actual expenses may be higher or lower than your initial projections, so track your expenses monthly to allow for adjustments. For instance, you may increase or decrease your marketing expenses according to projected costs versus actual expenses.

Labor

John and Mabel Smith share responsibility for buying, preparing and listing items, filling orders, and packing and shipping. Their son and daughter occasionally assist when needed and when Shuz N'Bags rents a table at antique fairs. A part-time bookkeeper and Web designer are contract workers.

Startup costs

John and Mabel Smith initially invested $2,000 to set up a website, register the business, set up accounts with online marketplaces and purchase the first items for inventory. In 2009, they invested another $2,000 of their retirement savings to purchase additional inventory. Financing for new purchases now comes from sales.

Funding requests

Shuz N'Bags is not seeking additional funding.

In this section, if you are going to borrow the money needed to start the business, you must provide a detailed financial statement in addition to the information already in your business plan. This is the same information you would provide for any substantial loan from a bank or other financial institution. You must provide assurance that you can and will pay back the loan and offer a form of security. This might be your home or other assets such as savings, stocks, or real estate. Your business and its assets will be part of the security package.

Many online sellers use personal credit cards to fund a business. If you have good personal credit and a high enough limit, you may be able to borrow the money from yourself. Be wary of high interest rates, and be sure you will be able to pay the monthly fees. Talk to your accountant and your banker about loan details. If you lend money to your company, you may be entitled to interest on the loan, as well as repayment.

Supporting Documents

Together with your business plan, keep copies of all official documents including business licenses, sales tax certificates, tax returns, contracts with consignment stores, loan documents, and year-end financial statements. Your business plan is an ongoing process, subject to changes and adjustments as you learn more about your business and make decisions that take it in new directions.

Glossary

3/5 year test: An objective IRS tax test that says an activity is a business if it generates a profit during at least three of the last five tax years, including the current year

12-month rule: Goods or services that last for 12 months or less

52-53 week tax year: A fiscal tax year that begins and ends with a specific day of the week and varies from 52 to 53 weeks

Accounting period: The period covered by your accounting system. For most small businesses, this is the same as the calendar year, January 1 through December 31 of every year.

Accounts payable: Expenses you have not yet paid out

Accounts receivable: Income that has not yet arrived in your possession

Adjusted basis: The original cost of an item plus certain additions, such as administration costs, and minus deductions, such as depreciation and casualty losses

Adjusted gross income (AGI): Your taxable income after all deductions have been taken

All-events test: A test used to determine whether a receipt or expense should be recorded in your accounts. The test is met when all the events that establish a financial obligation have occurred.

Alternative minimum tax (AMT): A parallel taxing system intended to ensure that wealthy individuals pay income tax

American Association for Retired Persons (AARP): A nonprofit, nonpartisan membership organization for people 50 and over

Annualized income installment method: A method for calculating quarterly income tax payments for seasonal or fluctuating income

Assets: Property you own or rent to carry on your business

Average markup percentage: The percentage you add to the wholesale price of an item to get its retail selling price

Balance sheet: A chart or document displaying your company's assets, liabilities, and equity, usually calculated from the time the business began to the present

Basis: The cost or purchase price of an item

Break-even: The point at which your income minus expenses is zero

Bright-line test: A clearly defined, objective standard or rule that leaves little or no room for interpretation

Business entity tax (BET): A flat annual fee levied on businesses in some states

Business plan: A concise written document that defines a business, its goals, and plans for achieving them

Capital expenses: The cost of business assets that have a useful life of more than one year

Constructive receipts: Money that has been made available to you "without substantial limitations" even though you do not yet have physical possession of it

Corporation: A business entity that has its own legal identity and is owned by shareholders and operated by a board of directors

Cost basis: What you paid to acquire an item

Cost method: A method of valuing inventory that tracks the purchase price of each item in your inventory plus any additional costs, such as shipping, storage, and repair

Credit card chargeback: A refund given to a customer by a credit card company

Dollar-value method: A method of pricing LIFO inventories by grouping goods and products into one or more pools (classes of items), depending on the kinds of goods or products in the inventories

Double taxation: Taxation of both a corporation and its shareholders on the earnings received from the corporation's business activities

Employer Identification Number (EIN): A number assigned by the IRS and used to identify the tax accounts of employers, certain sole proprietorships, corporations, and partnerships

Excise tax: A special tax on the sale of certain items, such as tobacco products, alcohol, and firearms

Expenses: The costs you incur in carrying on your business

Fair market value: The price at which an item would change hands between a buyer and a seller, when neither is forced to buy or sell, and both have reasonable knowledge of all necessary facts

Federal Unemployment Tax (FUTA): A payroll tax paid by employers into a federal fund that pays for the administration of state unemployment programs and extended unemployment benefits

First in, first out (FIFO): A method of valuing inventory that assumes the items you have purchased or produced first are the first items you sold, consumed, or otherwise disposed of

Fraud penalty: A penalty imposed by the IRS when a taxpayer deliberately underpays taxes; equal to 75 percent of the amount of the underpayment

Free file: An IRS program offering free online tax preparation and filing for individuals or married couples with an annual income of less than $58,000

Generally accepted accounting principles (GAAP): A generally accepted set of rules, conventions, standards, and procedures for reporting financial information established by the Financial Accounting Standards Board

Gross receipts: The total amounts of money you receive from all sources before accounting for expenses and losses

In-Kind Contribution: A charitable donation of property or goods

Income: Money coming in; also called a "credit" in accounting

Income statement: A simple statement showing your business income and expenses for a certain period, usually from the start of the most current accounting period to date

Individual Taxpayer Identification Number (ITIN): An identification number assigned by the IRS to an individual who otherwise would not qualify for a SSN but still needs such a number, such as an employer who is not a U.S. citizen or resident

Information return: An IRS form used to report certain payments made or received by your business

Internal Revenue Code (IRC): The body of U.S. law

that determines how taxes are calculated and paid

Internal Revenue Service (IRS): The U.S. federal agency responsible for collecting taxes and enforcing tax laws

Inventory: The value of all merchandise in your possession that is currently unsold

Ledger book: A bound set of blank sheets with preprinted grids of rows and columns, used for bookkeeping

Liabilities: Every item that is "owed" by your company including accounts payable, business loans, any bills from vendors or utilities, and funds in your possession that belong to others, such as income tax due to the state

Last in, first out (LIFO): A method of valuing inventory that assumes the items of inventory you purchased or produced last are sold or removed from inventory first

Maximum wage base: The maximum amount of wages and

earnings on which Social Security tax is paid

Modified Accelerated Cost Recovery System (MACRS): A method for calculating depreciation in which depreciation is evenly distributed over a lifespan assigned to each type of property by the IRS

Mortar-and-bricks: Having an actual building in a physical location for a business

Non-business debt: Debt that is not related to your business

Objective test: A test that defines criteria by examining objective facts, such as financial figures and specific time limits.

Offer in compromise (OIC): An agreement between a taxpayer and the IRS that settles the taxpayer's tax liabilities for less than the full amount owed

Ordinary loss: Losses incurred during the normal operation of a business

Owner's equity: Your assets minus your liabilities

Partnership: A business entity formed when two or more people get together and agree to carry on a business

Pass-through: A term referring to a business structure in which earnings pass through to the business owners and are taxed as personal income

Pease: An itemized deduction phase-out named after its author, Representative Donald Pease

Personal exemption phase-out (PEP): A phase out of the personal income tax exemption for high-income taxpayers

Populate: To enter data automatically in a spreadsheet or form through electronic updates

Profit: The point at which all income minus all expenses is greater than zero

Purchases account: A bookkeeping record of all items that you buy for your business and plan to resell to customers

Related person: A sibling, spouse, former spouse, child, grandchild or adopted child and their spouses

Required minimum withdrawal (RMD): The amount you must withdraw every year from a traditional IRA after you turn 70 ½.

Retail method: A method of valuing inventory by subtracting the mark-up percentage from total sales

S corporation: Small business corporation, a corporation that elects to pass corporate income, losses, deductions and credit through to its shareholders for federal tax purposes and has fewer than 100 shareholders

Scientific wild-ass guess (SWAG): A U.S. Army acronym for an estimate based on all available information

Simplified dollar-value method: A system of inventory valuation that uses changes in the price index to estimate the annual change in price of classes of inventory items

Social Security Administration (SSA): The U.S. government agency responsible for administering the Social Security program

Social Security number (SSN): A nine-digit identification number assigned by the SSA to U.S. citizens, permanent residents, and temporary (working) residents under section 205(c)(2) of the Social Security Act, codified as 42 U.S.C. § 405(c)(2)

Sole proprietorship: A type of business entity owned and operated by one individual.

Substantial understatement of income exception: An exception to the usual three-year deadline for initiating an audit that allows the IRS to conduct an audit if the amount of income omitted on a tax return exceeds 25 percent of the income reported on that return

Tax gap: The amount of taxes that is not paid each year because taxpayers underreport their income

Tax Identification Number (TIN): A nine-digit number assigned to trusts, fiduciaries, and other nonbusiness entities by the IRS for tax purposes. A SSN is the TIN for individuals, and an EIN is the TIN for corporations, partnerships, and sole proprietorships that employ workers.

Tax year: The 12-month period over which your taxes are calculated

Trade assistant: An online seller who helps other individuals sell their items

Universal Commercial Code (UCC): An initiative to standardize the laws governing sales and other commercial transactions in all 50 states

Worthless debt: Debt that can be shown to be uncollectible

Bibliography

Barton, Stephanie. "7 most overlooked tax deductions." MSNBC. January 1, 2010. **www.msnbc.msn.com/id/34961179/ns/business-personal_finance/t/most-overlooked-tax-deductions.**

Crenshaw, Albert B. "Higher-Income Benefits Fade." *Washington Post.* Feb. 26, 2006. **www.washingtonpost.com/wp-dyn/content/article/2006/02/25/AR2006022500249.html.**

Delafuente, Charles. "Selling on eBay? Keep Eye on Gains." *The New York Times.* February 10, 2008. **www.nytimes.com/2008/02/10/business/yourtaxes/10ebay.html.**

"Do You Have to Pay Sales Tax on Internet Purchases?" Findlaw.com. **http://smallbusiness.findlaw.com/business-operations/internet/internet-taxes.html.**

Dun & Bradstreet. "Determining Whether to Use Cash or Accrual Accounting." **http://smallbusiness.dnb.com/company-activities-management/financial-performance/12313771-1.html.**

Ely, Bruce P., Christopher R. Grissom, and William T. Thistle. State Tax Treatment of LLCs and LLPs — 2011 Update. Tax Analysts. **www.babc.com/files/Publication/5ac35bb5-2520-4e20-a88f-**

99bb519612fd/Presentation/PublicationAttachment/2c86a094-89f2-4729-831f-a617a7eaa89e/Ely.pdf.

Fawkner, Elena. "Taxation 101: Hobby or Business?" AHBBO. 2001. **www.ahbbo.com/hobbybusiness.html.**

Fleenor, Patrick. *Fixing the Alternative Minimum Tax: AMT Reform Requires Changes to Regular Tax Code. Special Report No. 155.* Tax Foundation. May 17, 2007. **www.taxfoundation.org/news/show/22400.html.**

_____. *PEP and Pease: Repealed for 2010 But Preparing a Comeback. Special Report No. 178.* Tax Foundation. April 29, 2010. **www.taxfoundation.org/publications/show/26260.html.**

Hagen, K. M. "How To Account for Inventory for Income Tax Purposes." GoogoBits.com. September 1, 2005. **www.googobits.com/articles/2400-how-to-account-for-inventory-for-income-tax-purposes.html.**

Hicks, Greta P., CPA. "What To Do If The IRS Audits Your Tax Return." Uncle Fed's Tax Board.com. 2005. **www.unclefed.com/AuthorsRow/GretaHicks/audit.html.**

Holden, Greg. "Main Street Fairness Act May Be Taxing for Online Merchants." AuctionBytes.com. April 28, 2009. **www.auctionbytes.com/cab/abn/y09/m04/i28/s00.**

If You Are Self-Employed. SSA Publication No. 05-10022, January 2011, ICN 454900. **www.ssa.gov/pubs/10022.html.**

Internet Sales Tax Fairness. New Rules Project. **www.newrules.org/retail/rules/internet-sales-tax-fairness.**

Inventory — Manufacturing Tax Tips. IRS.gov. **www.irs.gov/businesses/small/industries/article/0,,id=100355,00.html.**

Jopson, Barney. "Online sales tax battle looms in US." *Financial Times.*
FT.com. June 12, 2011. **www.ft.com/intl/cms/s/0/2e2cd154-9526-
11e0-a648-00144feab49a.html#axzz1PM6HJ26A.**

Kopytoff, Verne G. "Amazon Pressured on Sales Tax."
The New York Times. March 13, 2011.
www.nytimes.com/2011/03/14/technology/14amazon.html.

Metz, Rachel. "EBay 4Q revenue rises, helped by holiday shoppers."
Physorg.com. January 19, 2011. **www.physorg.com/news/2011-01-
ebay-4q-revenue-holiday-shoppers.html.**

Murray, Jean. "Can My Business Deduct Charitable Contributions?"
About.com. **http://biztaxlaw.about.com/od/businesstaxdeduction1/f/
charitydeducts.htm.**

Sales Tax on the Internet. Nolo.com.
www.nolo.com/legal-encyclopedia/sales-tax-internet-29919.html.

Social Security & Medicare Tax Rates. Social Security Online: Trust Fund
Data. **www.socialsecurity.gov/oact/ProgData/taxRates.html.**

Tax Laws and Issues — E-Business & E-Commerce. Internal
Revenue Service. **www.irs.gov/businesses/small/industries/
article/0,,id=209348,00.html.**

Watson, Rick. "6 Things I Learned at the Amazon Annual Shareholder
Meeting." Rick Watson's Blog. 2010. **http://rickwatson.tumblr.
com/2010-amazon-annual-shareholder-meeting/.**

What Is The Difference Between Earned, Portfolio, And Passive Income?
**www.taxbraix.com/tax-articles/difference-between-earned-portfolio-
passive-income.html.**

Author Biography

Martha Maeda is author of several books on personal finance, including *The Complete Guide to Investing in Bonds and Bond Funds, The Complete Guide to IRAs and IRA Investing, Retire Rich with Your Roth IRA, Roth 401(k) and Roth 403(b),* and *Wipe Out Your Student Loans and Be Debt Free Fast!* After graduating from Northwestern University, she lived and worked in Australia, Japan, and several African countries before settling with her family in Orlando, Florida. She is particularly interested in the growth of e-commerce, which has allowed  individuals to achieve economic success working from their home offices and created new careers and new ways of doing business.

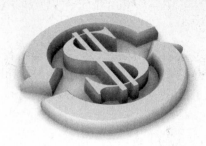

Index